Implementation and Management of Performance Improvement Plans

Emphasizing Group and Organizational Interventions

Robert Carleton

HRD Press, Inc. • Amherst • Massachusetts

Published by: HRD Press, Inc.
22 Amherst Road
Amherst, MA 01002
800-822-2801 (U.S. and Canada)
413-253-3488
413-253-3490 (fax)
www.hrdpress.com

ISBN 978-1-59996-188-0

Production services by Jean Miller
Editorial services by Suzanne Bay, Sally Farnham
Cover design by Eileen Klockars

Table of Contents

Introduction

This book is about the Implementation phase of Performance Improvement—the "how to get desired results and payoffs" phase of Human Performance Technology (HPT). It is, of course, in the Implementation phase that reality strikes. The analysis and design that precede implementation are all theoretical until this phase is successfully completed and intended results delivered.

Planning is a substitute for depending on "good luck," and this phase is where something useful happens, or doesn't.

Implementation is a "mid-process" activity in performance improvement, and as such, success in this phase is *highly* dependent on the adequacy of the analysis and design that have preceded this activity. In other words, *this book begins with the assumption that a proper and thorough analysis has already been completed, and on the basis of this analysis, an "informed" and targeted performance plan (or statement of intent) has been developed. With this design in hand, you are now ready to implement.*

While the intent of the author is to address the area of implementation of performance improvement plans broadly, there will undeniably be more attention given to performance plans focused on larger scale implementations—efforts aimed at group, groups of groups, and enterprise-wide performance issues.

The reason for this is simple: a lot has been written already by many others on systematic approaches to individual performance improvement and comparatively very little regarding systematic and systemic group through enterprise interventions. There are some fundamental differences between dealing with performance on an individual level versus groups of performers whose activities are interdependent requiring them to work in coordination, or alignment, to achieve the desired result. Further, there are some pretty basic misconceptions and errors made by many when they move from an individual focus to a group focus.

I have heard more than once from highly respected and competent colleagues that when it comes to achieving outstanding performance focusing on individuals or on entire large enterprises, it is all the same thing—it is "just a matter of scale."

I will grant that, arguably, if you step back far enough and focus on large overarching principles, that statement may well be true. However, when you get into the trenches of implementing a performance improvement plan that involves the coordinated efforts of hundreds, or even thousands, of individual performers scattered across multiple functions, units, and often locations, it sure looks and feels quite different from individually focused performance improvement actions.

One of the key differences can be most simply summed up in what might, at first glance, appear to be an attempt on the author's part to make a "cute" or flamboyant statement:

> Never lose sight of the fact that when dealing with group and multiple group performance the improvement plan you have in hand when you begin the implementation phase will represent something between at worst a WAG (wild a** guess) and at *best* a SWAG (scientific wild a** guess).

Which of these two you actually have—a SWAG or a WAG—will be dependent on the quality of the preceding analysis and design. An analysis and design based on a systematic body of knowledge, rooted in a deep understanding of "system" will give you a SWAG that is robust enough to carry you through the inherent iterative nature of system interventions where evaluation, further analysis, design alteration, and repeated modification of various elements of the plan are all going on simultaneously as you claw your way through, in what often feels like chaos, to eventual organizational performance improvement.

Without a robust analysis and design based on a systematic body of knowledge, you will have a WAG, and the failure of your endeavor is almost assured as you will not be prepared to adequately react to the inevitable "new data" that will present itself requiring you to react "on the fly" as you pursue your intended organizational improvement.

When implementing a performance plan at group and organizational levels, it is very helpful to keep in mind the words of Field Marshal Ferdinand Foch from the First World War: "No plan survives contact with the enemy." The complex realities of organizations with their internal inter-relations combined with the highly changing external environment in a steadily globalizing economy make "dead accurate and thoroughly complete" performance plans at group and organizational levels an unachievable ideal. The larger the entity of focus, the greater the flexibility required for success when implementation begins. Implementation must be viewed as an iterative process—self correcting through comparing progress with objectives. The larger the entity of focus, the greater the criticality of having an effective iterative process that ensures that the *eventual* results of the effort match the original, or revised, intent. And, this matching of intent to result must occur without also creating unanticipated problems/downsides elsewhere in the organization (as well as outside the organization with external clients and our shared society) that offset or neutralize the gains.

Regardless of the "level" of performance plan implementation (individual, group, organization, societal) at the core of effective Implementation are two underlying principles that must be kept in mind throughout the phase. These are the principles of System and Alignment. In addition to these two underpinning principles are two knowledge/skill areas that are critical for successful Implementation; these are the areas of Change Management and Project Management.

With a clear understanding of System and Alignment, the performance technologist applies the skills and knowledge of Change Management and Project Management to ensure that there is both Clarity about what is expected as well as the Ability to perform. These are the underpinnings that enable you to Achieve Sustained Results.

This book is organized around the six topic areas indicated above:

1. System
2. Alignment
3. Change Management
4. Project Management
5. Ensuring Clarity and Ability
6. Achieving Sustained Results

System

We were born into and live, work, and die within a System. Having an impact on human performance means working with a System. Granted, we are usually limiting our performance focus to one or more subsystems, but this does not change the fact that we must be broadly systemic in our analysis, design, and Implementation if we expect to be successful; systemic in adding value to all stakeholders, inside and outside our organization.

The concepts of System, component subsystems, and then being systemic have been dealt with in an earlier book in this series. However, the concept of System and being systemic is so critical to effective Implementation that I will do a relatively quick review of these basics with a focus on the implications of both in regard to successful Implementation.

While there are "errors" one can make in the Implementation process itself, by far the bulk of failures are simply the predictable result of poor or inadequate planning, analysis, and/or design. In my experience, the root cause of most of this faulty analysis and/or design can be attributed to an inadequate and/or blocked ability to deal with the realities of System thinking, planning, and consequences.

Alignment

Alignment is about balance, linking, and focus within a System (or subsystem) to achieve some stated valuable objective. One of the professional groups that focus on organizational alignment has defined Alignment as "coherence of effort across the organization." We would add "to add measurable value to all internal and external partners."

Another one of the primary characteristics of System is the idea of accommodation and linking across subsystems. Elements of a system must be able and willing to accommodate their own desires to better balance with the desires of those around them with whom they have to interact. Interface points between identifiable subsystems must be points of mutual give-and-take if the system is to be maximally effective.

There are those in the performance improvement field, including this author, who would contend that successful Implementation of a performance improvement initiative is all about alignment. This is particularly true when dealing with performance improvement applied to groups and organizations. Alignment is arguably the single most important issue for successful implementation providing lasting and useful results.

Change Management

Change Management is also a fundamental aspect of Implementation. This topic by itself has generated many books and papers. There will be no attempt to thoroughly cover all aspects of Change Management. What will be covered here are the central elements of Change Management, the critical "dynamic" aspects that are central to the Implementation phase.

Out of all the Change Management theory, research, and experience, there are four fundamental characteristics of effective change efforts that must be continuously incorporated and applied throughout the Implementation process:

1. Increase the benefit to all stakeholders
2. Reduce and eliminate the uncertainty and threat
3. Deliver clarity
4. Diminish the effort

These four are continuous actions that must permeate all aspects of the implementation process.

Further there are some aspects of Change Management that have come to be viewed differently over the past 30 years:

- There are now different approaches for participative change and declarative change.

- There are incremental changes and transformational changes, each with its own patterns and processes.

- Change is now considered endemic to business and society in general rather than the occasional project.

- And through all of this, the requirement for speed in accomplishing desired changes has increased.

All of these change issues are worthy of note here, again focusing on the impact on Implementation and the consequences of what is delivered.

Project Management

The last area of specific knowledge that is often critical to successful Implementation is Project Management. While this is a topic that has *not* been covered in an earlier volume in this series, it is none the less a field of knowledge on which much has been written. Project Management can be a profession all by itself and is the activity that stitches everything together as one moves from Planning through Implementation to value added.[1]

One of the places in which Performance Improvement Implementation is somewhat different from "traditional" Project Management is in the highly iterative nature of group and organizational performance improvement initiatives—which make many of the later project tasks and activities virtually unknown during the planning phases. It is not uncommon, particularly in large-scale transformations, to build in further Analysis and Design activities (often done by the target population or representatives of it) as part and parcel of the overall implementation.

The larger the target system of the performance intervention, the more potentially complex the situation. Complexity in organizations often means that some aspects of the performance may not be visible at the beginning of the project. For example, if the initial Analysis indicates that the performers are unaware of the necessity to engage in some aspects of the target performance, it will obviously not be performed. In this case, the initial intervention is to inform the target population of the necessity. Once the desired performance is clearly understood by the performers, the investigator may discover that

---

[1] There will be no attempt to be definitive on that subject within this book. In a like manner to the above topics, I will cover some limited aspects of project management solely in regard to Performance Improvement Implementation.

there are other impediments to adequate performance that were not visible until after the desired performance was made clear. The situation can indeed be a bit like peeling the proverbial onion. As you resolve each impediment to desired performance, previously unknown issues may arise. The performance technologist has to dig through and resolve each element progressively (an iterative approach) until eventually the desired performance is achieved.

All of this also leads into another "common" issue the performance technologist may have with Project Management—or more correctly the project manager with whom the performance technologist has been assigned to work.

Project managers are often specially trained and certified in Project Management. This training is often (always in my own experience) focused on traditional projects—such as plant maintenance—and does not take into account the nature of change in both living systems in general and human beings specifically. As stated above, changing performance is often like peeling an onion with successive layers of issues pertaining to and having a bearing on performance levels.

In traditional Project Management, when elements of the project are somewhat uncertain or become vague, the traditional Project Management is trained to drive hard to increased detail and clarity—in effect greater and greater detail is the answer to uncertainty. This is, unfortunately, not the appropriate path in group and organizational performance improvement. In these iterative situations, the most appropriate approach is to build in clarification processes—not greater detail initially, but processes designed to surface greater detail—often, additional investigation/analysis that is done by the target population.

Ensuring Clarity and Ability

The first active step in implementing a performance improvement plan is to ensure that the person or population being targeted by the plan, and any others who have a direct or indirect impact on that target and/or the ability to implement the plan, are fully aware of what is intended and how it applies to them. It should come as no shock that awareness and focus on useful results must precede taking action.

Until this Clarity is achieved, it is often impossible to ascertain whether or not the target has the Ability to perform as desired. By Ability, I mean are they both able and allowed to perform as desired or are there

- skill deficiencies
- resource restraints
- environmental restraints
- conflicting behaviors that have higher value

How this ensuring of Clarity and Ability is best done varies based on the nature of the work and whether the target is an individual, a team, a group of teams, or an entire organization.

Achieving Sustained Results

Making people aware of what is desired and ensuring that they have the Ability to perform as desired is the enabler to achieving the "holy grail" of performance improvement, which is a sustained result as desired. There are a number of factors involved in achieving this end result and these include the following:

- The ability of the target to measure and track their own progress

- Support subsystems that make it easier—more rewarding—to change than not change

- Supportive actions on the part of those "around" the target

- The target believing in the value and importance of performing as desired

  - The "social" group believing in the value/importance
  - The observed consequences of changing and not changing

    - Support and follow-through by immediate supervision

- The value placed on the change by the organization and how it signals that value

- The value added within and outside the organization

It is also important that the "results" of a systemic performance improvement plan have two broad types of measurable results as indicated in the quote below, otherwise the result is not systemic and potential success is seriously jeopardized, particularly in organizational settings. The best *complete* definition of "results" I have seen is embedded in a quote from William Pasmore, one of the founding fathers of *Socieotechnical Systems*.

Effective organizations are those which deliver excellent results by any measure of cost, quality, or efficiency, while simultaneously enhancing the energy and commitment of the members of the organization to the success of the enterprise.

This quotation provides another way of thinking about results, particularly in the organizational context. Any performance plan—be it aimed at an individual, a group of individuals, a team, a group of teams, or an entire organization—should have built into it two primary properties, both of which can be measured:

- It should result in measurable improvements in some measure or measures of cost, quality, or efficiency.

- It should measurably increase the energy and commitment of the targets of the plan to the success of the enterprise and all of its stakeholders.

If the performance plan does not deliver *both,* it is not systemic, and sustained impact becomes highly questionable.

And then there is the final piece of sustained performance today that represents a notable shift from previous thoughts around organizational Change. In years past, the model of Change incorporated the concepts of first unfreezing the System, making the change, and then **refreezing** the System. This piece is no longer appropriate. Change is coming so fast and so continuously today that the concept of refreezing no longer applies.

Effective organizations today must incorporate continuous change—or Continuous Improvement—into their organizational value system and make continuous Change part of their way of life. This book is organized around these six broad topics: System, Alignment, Change Management, Project Management, Ensuring Clarity and Ability, Achieving Sustained Results. This is supplemented by appendices in an attempt to provide helpful examples and some useful tools.

Professional Standards

Finally, it is important to note that of the ten standards for performance improvement, as described by the International Society for Performance Improvement and the American Society of Training and Development, eight are fundamental to the implementation process (indicated in bold) and another is a constant underpinning (indicated in bold italics). These standards are:

1. *Focus on results and help clients focus on results.*

2. **Look at situations systemically taking into consideration the larger context, including competing pressures, resource constraints, and anticipated change.**

3. **Add value in how you do the work and through the work itself.**

4. **Utilize partnerships or collaborate with clients and other experts as required.**

5. Be systematic in all aspects of the process, including the assessment of the need or opportunity.

6. **Be systematic in all aspects of the process, including the analysis of the work and workplace to identify the cause or factors that limit performance.**

7. **Be systematic in all aspects of the process, including the design of the solution or specification of the requirements of the solution.**

8. **Be systematic in all aspects of the process, including the development of all or some of the solution and its elements.**

9. **Be systematic in all aspects of the process, including the implementation of the solution.**

10. **Be systematic in all aspects of the process, including the evaluation of the process and the results (both internal and external).**

Now, let me go back and make sure I have put a stake firmly in the ground on one point. Standards 6 through 10 all begin with the statement "Be systematic in all aspects of the process including..."

According to *Webster's International Unabridged Dictionary,* a synonym for *systematic* is *orderly.* Of the initial three definitions of systematic, which cover the most common uses of the word, two are centered on the "orderly" aspect of systematic.

Following on from comments made above regarding the differences between individual performance plans and those aimed at "groups" of performers through enterprise-wide interventions—systemic interventions into performance issues involving groups of performers **are rarely, if ever, orderly**. The larger the entity you are focusing on, the more iterative and chaotic the implementation process will become.

The only definition of *systematic* that applies in larger scale performance interventions is definition 1b:

b : reduced to or presented or formulated as a coherent body of ideas or principles : offering or constituting a complete scheme, outline, or classification <*systematic* philosophical thought>

There is indeed a coherent body of ideas or principles that constitute a complete scheme that the competent performance technologist will bring to bear on performance issues—and in that sense **systematic** is indeed critical and characteristic of being competent in this field. But this systematic body of principles will almost never be played out in an **orderly** manner.

If you wish to be successful in dealing with performance issues beyond the performance of individuals dealt with one at a time, when it comes to Implementation, never confuse *systematic* with *orderly*. You could, however, substitute *systemically* for *systematic* in Standards 1 through 6 and I, for one, would heartily agree.

Chapter 1
System

We are born into and live, work, and die within a System. Trying to have an impact on human performance means working within a System, which is why the second of the ten standards for Performance Improvement is "look at situations systemically. "While it is true that usually you will be limiting your performance focus on any given project to one or more subsystems, this does not change the fact that to be effective, you have to be broadly systemic in your Analysis, Design, and Implementation if you expect to be successful; you have to align everything that is used, done, produced, and delivered to external clients and society.

The concepts of System, subsystems, and being systemic have been dealt with in earlier books in this series. However, the concept of System and being systemic is so critical to effective Implementation that I will do a relatively quick review of these basics with a focus on the implications of both in regard to Implementation.

While there are many "errors" one can make in the Implementation process itself, by far the bulk of failures that I have seen are simply the predictable result of poor or inadequate analysis and/or design. In my experience, the root cause of most of this faulty analysis and/or design can be attributed to a failure to fully and adequately deal with the realities of System.

An oft repeated phrase, and one that most managers will at least superficially agree with, is "an organization is a System." Rarely heard, at least in my experience, is *why* this view is held, or even more importantly, what the consequences of this are for management and general organizational performance. Given the context of Implementation of an HPT plan, it is worthwhile to take the time to cover both of these bits of reality.

The definition of *System* from *Webster's Unabridged Dictionary* is as follows:

1 a : a complex unity formed of many often diverse parts subject to a common plan or serving a common purpose **b :** an aggregation or assemblage of objects joined in regular interaction or interdependence : a set of units combined by nature or art to form an integral, organic, or organized whole : an orderly working totality : a coherent unification.

– "system." *Webster's Third New International Dictionary, Unabridged.* Merriam-Webster, 2002.

A business organization is indeed a collection of different units, each with a particular function or functions, that when working together accomplish some business purpose (including adding value to all stakeholders) that none of the elements operating on their own could accomplish.

The same is true of nonprofit groups, governmental agencies, or any group of people coming together for some common purpose. But to take it a bit further, even an individual, operating in isolation, is an "organic" system and all the rules of system theory apply.

The crux of implementation is in acting systemically, which requires System awareness, System thinking, and System sensitivity in Design and Implementation.[1]

While System theory has many aspects, I will limit this discussion of system theory to the elements that have a direct bearing on Implementation. The basic definition of a System is that it is a set of two or more elements that satisfy the following three conditions:

1. *The behavior of each element of a System has an effect on the performance of the whole System.* Nothing in an organization happens in isolation. Whatever happens in one area has an impact on other areas. An obvious example that HR departments often spend hours on is how individual staff are handled in terms of absences, vacation days, pay, grievances, performance management, etc. How things like these are done in one part of an organization has an impact on all other areas in terms of perceptions, expectations, and potentially morale if nothing else.

One of the key Implementation issues deriving from this aspect of System theory is that whatever the target or focus for the HPT plan, there will be implications/ impact on other units or areas in the organization. Obviously the degree or amount of impact is not uniform across the entire system. It will vary—often as a function of "operational" distance from the area being targeted for a Performance Improvement effort. What I mean by operational distance is in terms of the work flow. For example, changes in decisions made about credit can have a significant impact on the collections function, increasing or decreasing the collections activity as a direct result of the "credit" actions. At the same time, activities in the shipping department or in vendor relations may not be perceptibly impacted, at least in the short term, by those same decisions made in the credit department. However, over the long term, those credit decisions could eventually have a significant impact on the nature and/or perceptions of the customer base that could then begin to perceptibly impact activities in places like shipping and vendor relations.

The issue for Implementation is being aware of the potential for impact in areas of the organization that are not directly targeted by the HPT plan you are implementing. If there is an impact, there will be a reaction, and how will the reaction play out in the organization overall and between the various groups in the organization? Those reactions can be at the center of success or failure of the HPT initiative.

2. *The behavior of the elements of the system and their effects on the whole System are interdependent.* In other words, the overall organizational System has an impact on the performance of each piece of the System, and the pieces of the System have an impact on the whole System. In a single work unit, you can see the same phenomena in the group dynamics. The individuals have an impact on the group, and the group likewise has an impact on each individual.

When considering the potential impact of the HPT initiative on the rest of the System, the implementer also has to keep in mind that for every action there is a reaction. Any area that is impacted will react in some manner, and that reaction will have an impact on the entity targeted by the HPT initiative. These types of "action—reaction—reaction" are all things that the implementer has to consider, track, and monitor as the Implementation process proceeds.

3. *However subgroups of the elements are formed, each has an effect on the behavior of the whole and none has an independent effect on it.* This means that no matter how you organize the parts of a System, you cannot isolate the System impact and further it is always a two way street—each element impacts the System and the System impacts each element no matter how you organize it.

This is a somewhat elegant way of saying that there is no getting around the systemic nature of a System. The idea of buffering or walling off some aspect of the System for "independent" action is fundamentally unsound. Many would in fact say that attempting to do so is a fool's errand. You should not waste time to isolate or "cordon off" the impact; the focus must be on accommodation and incorporation of these impacts into the overall plan. Working these elements into the plan is the primary responsibility of the person or persons doing the Design, which is in turn dependent on a System-sensitive Analysis. The management and tracking of these impacts as you proceed with Implementation, as well as any adjustments or modifications to the Implementation as a result of these impacts, is a primary responsibility of the implementer or Implementation team.

The concept of an individual performer in an organization being a part of, and working within, a system seems to be generally understood and accepted by most Performance Improvement implementers. But when the object of focus becomes a group, unit, department, or entire function, this awareness seems to drop off considerably. This is probably tied to the drop off in "obviousness" of the System phenomena. When observing one person's performance within a group of workers, it is not a stretch to realize that many things are not within the control of the individual performer and that the other people with whom the individual works will have an impact on the performance of the individual. When dealing with a group of people, a unit, or an entire function, it is relatively easy to think the "group" in question is self-contained. Even the manner of graphically representing groups on an organization chart implies that each box is somewhat independent with "space" between them and any other group. The reality of the situation is that the system nature of groups within an organization is a direct extension of the same concepts.

In terms of implementing a performance plan and being sensitive to the system implications of the performance plan, let me start with the individual and work up to groups. Individual performance is the result of the interactions of a number of System variables—all of which must be understood and either addressed or consciously discarded as not relevant in any particular Performance Improvement plan.

Performance Standards/Specifications

Is the desired performance and the standards to which it must be performed documented anywhere? And if so, is the performer aware of them, have access to them, understand them, and believe that attaining the standards is possible and reasonable?

It should come as no great surprise that individual performance delivered on the day will reflect what the performer feels is expected, possible, and reasonable. But to get a real understanding of the systemic nature of performance, let's go through how you check on ensuring that performance standards and specifications are adequately covered:

- Do standards exist? Ask the performer, and if he or she is uncertain, you have to find out who has responsibility for specifying the performance and facilitate ways for this information to get codified and communicated.

- Are the standards rigorous and ideally measured in terms of measurable indicators?
- Are the standards based on valid criteria?
- Is the performer aware of the standards? This part is easy: you ask the performer.
- Does the performer understand the standards? Again, ask the performer to describe the desired performance and standards.
- Is the performer's understanding accurate? This is obviously something you cannot ask the performer. You are once again required to go to another source or sources in the organization to ascertain the accuracy of the performer's understanding.
- Does the performer believe the standards are attainable and reasonable? Now we are back to simply asking the performer. But suppose the answer to this question is negative; in that case, you are going to have to include other people in the organization to work through the attainability and reasonableness of the performance specifications.

Performance Resources

Is there sufficient time, are the available tools adequate, is there sufficient staff, and is there sufficient information to enable appropriate performance? If the answer to *any* of these is no, remediation of the problems is generally not within the control of the individual performer. Deficiencies in these areas will clearly impact on individual performance, yet dealing with deficiencies in these areas requires the HPT practitioner to look into the System beyond the individual performer.

Performance Support

Here is an interesting relationship between the perception of "support" or "non-support" in the work place and any physical support tools that may or may not be available. While there is indeed a case to be made for physical evidence of support for performing the job—such as job aids, references, coaches, samples, and such—there is also a desire on the part of most workers to "feel" supported. Feeling supported is an emotional requirement and, as such, is not necessarily a "logical" issue that is easily determined by looking for the presence of physical support tools such as job aids, references, and samples. I have, in fact, more than once come across situations where the presence of physical support tools was interpreted by the incumbents as evidence of *lack* of support. If I take a simple job aid designed to guide task performance in real time as an example, there are two basic ways the mere presence of this job aid can be interpreted as evidence of lack of support.

1. "This task is not considered important enough for the supervisor to spend any time with us or otherwise be bothered when we are assigned this duty." If the job aid is viewed as a means to keep the supervisor from "having to bother" with people who are performing the task, it can be viewed as evidence of non-support, or a non-valued job.

2. "Using this job aid makes me feel like some two year old who can't be trusted to do even simple things correctly." If the job aid is considered to be overly simplistic, demeaning, or "talking down to us" in its content, it can leave people performing the task feeling that the organization considers them to be a "lower class" group that is not even minimally competent. Feeling that you are looked "down on" with some lower level of competence from "normal" people does not engender feelings of support in the job.

The perception people may hold regarding performance support tools clearly has ties to perceptions of management and supervision—and, in this case, with the manner in which the job aid may have been presented and/or commented on by the supervisor or manager of the unit.

This brings us to the often far more difficult issue of feelings of "support" that are directly tied to the nature and demeanor of the supervision and/or management of the job and people doing the job.

It is not particularly unusual (not the norm fortunately, but still not unusual) when doing an analysis of a problem to have someone in a work unit pop out with some form of sarcastic greeting that lets you know he or she does not feel valued or supported. "Welcome to F Troop," "So what can the legion of the lost do for you?" and "You don't want to hang around here too long or you will end up like us. Everyone else will forget you even exist," are all examples of statements I have heard. All of these statements relate most directly to what they see and hear from the immediate supervision and management of the area.

Heskett and Sasser in their work on the *Service Profit Chain* have documented this same phenomenon and its impact on customer retention as has W. Warner Burke in his work and research on customer satisfaction. To loosely paraphrase both bodies of work, "the service that front line people deliver to the customer will be a reflection of the service these front line people feel they are getting from both their management and the organization for which they work."

Another area of support that is often overlooked in Implementation plans is around supporting self-management. Does the organization provide sufficient information about the task to enable people to self-manage around the task? Self-management relates primarily to the ability of the task performer to anticipate and plan for performing the task, as well as the ability to ascertain how well the task has been done when completed or when in process. The more people are able to self-manage the initiation and appropriate completion of a task, the less inclined they will be to feel demeaned or overlooked—both of which can have a direct and measurable impact on quantity and quality of jobs done. If the performer is unaware of when a performance is required and/or is unable to ascertain the degree to which the job is done satisfactorily it can indeed be a problem in terms of performing.

The potential impact of any of these support issues on the performance of the individual worker is not hard to understand once considered. And it should be equally obvious that if there are problems in this area, the performance specialist will have to look beyond the individual performer for both causes and solutions—these reside elsewhere in the system and not with the individual performer.

Performance Interference

Are there things going on that actively interfere with the ability of the individual performer to actually engage in the tasks in question? If other tasks are interfering, it raises the question of why, and can this be changed—which will often involve checking/ negotiating with others in the organization.

Likewise, job procedures and work flows that are considered illogical, clumsy, or irrelevant by the person performing a given task can actively interfere with the ability to perform to standard. Issues surrounding performance interference will rarely have been developed by, or be in control of, the person or persons doing the task. So once again you are lead elsewhere in the organization for possible solutions.

Performance Consequences

Are the consequences for performance aligned to support and deliver the desired performance? Are the consequences meaningful from the performer's viewpoint? And are consequences for performance delivered or available in a timely manner?

In most instances, the formal delivery of consequences for performance, be they positive or negative, are done by the immediate supervisor or manager. In the instance of a self-directed work team, they may be in the hands of the performer's fellow workers. Little if any of this rests in the hands of the individual performer. And when it comes to "informal" delivery of consequences, it can come from any number of sources—supervisors, managers, fellow workers, customers, vendors, etc. We may be trying to figure out why a performance being delivered by a particular person is what it is, but we cannot understand the performance consequences component by focusing on the performer alone.

There are many examples of this type of problem, and rarely does the understanding and resolution of a performance consequences problem rest with the individual performer.

I came across a classic example of this when investigating why there was so little compliance with a mandated diversity program for a large national retailer. The assumption was that there was some sort of hidden or buried discrimination issue on the part of store managers. The reality turned out to be far more prosaic than the assumed insidious nature of hidden discrimination. In fact, when given a paired comparison rating across all store manager tasks, the diversity issue was considered quite high in the priority ratings.

The source of the problem was far more mundane. The amount of time a store manager got with his or her zone supervisor had been steadily diminishing over the previous 10 years as part of the continual efforts on efficiency and cost control, which resulted in considerably enlarged "spans of control" for each zone manager. It was now generally agreed that zone supervisors had insufficient time to deal with all the factors involved in store performance. With limited time in the store, zone managers focused on those things that had the most direct bearing on how they (the zone managers) would personally be evaluated by *their* supervisors. So if issues that impacted on the rating of the zone supervisor were not done appropriately by the store manager, there were immediate consequences in the form of a displeased zone manager. Diversity targets were considered primarily a store issue as the store manager did the hiring and firing—not the zone supervisor.

This meant that the only time there were any negative consequences to the store manager for not moving forward on the diversity issue was in the annual performance review when the zone supervisor's task was systematically reviewing the performance of the store manager against the store manager responsibilities. The nature of the System dictated that in the weekly meetings with the zone manager for at least 11 months of the year, diversity goals were "out of site and out of mind"— effectively consequence free in what was otherwise a consequence rich environment.

The unintended message to the store manager was loud and clear: "There are lots to be focusing on and you better be doing it." But diversity was not important enough to the zone manager and the organization to even talk about it other than once a year.

Performance Feedback

Does the performer receive information about his or her performance? And if they do receive information, is it relevant, accurate, timely, specific, and easy to understand?

This is an area that routinely comes up when evaluating why there is deficient performance delivered, even though it is clear there are no skill or knowledge deficiencies that account for the problem.

Performance feedback is one of the most misunderstood areas of Performance Management that I have encountered in my 30 years of working performance issues. Performance feedback problems are yet another area of the system where the analysis and resolution of problems rest outside of the individual performer.

Performance feedback must be

- relevant,
- accurate,
- timely,
- specific,
- easy to understand.

Relevant. Performance feedback is information that is both actionable and meaningful with clear and immediate ties to the performance and the performance standards. Feedback should not be obtuse, conceptual, or quizzical. The information provided and its tie to the performance being commented on must be immediately clear to the recipient of the feedback.

Accurate. Performance feedback should not be an estimate or supposition, nor based on someone else's perception with which the performer disagrees but cannot discuss with the actual observer of the behavior. It has to be an accurate objective reflection of what actually occurred.

Timely. The definition of *timely* is *immediately useful to the performer.* For my money herein lies one of the greatest problems today in terms of effectively supervising and managing task behavior. I can think of no other area with more inaccurate information and inaccurate interpretation than the area of timeliness of feedback.

It must be remembered that a key criteria for feedback is that it must be immediately useful to the performer. To be immediately useful, the performer must be able to apply or utilize the feedback immediately. There are two types of data that a performer can receive in terms of performance feedback:

1. Information that is intended to either increase or decrease the likelihood of exhibiting that behavior again. This is generally referred to as motivational feedback.

2. Information that is intended to modify the form or nature of the behavior the next time it is exhibited. This is generally referred to as formative feedback or coaching/counseling.

The problem here is that functionally the proper timing of these two types of feedback is quite different. Motivational feedback, which is designed to increase or decrease the likelihood of exhibiting that behavior, again, has to be delivered immediately following the performance. If I do something well and it is commented on immediately after I do it, I feel good about the performance and will most likely engage in that behavior again, in the same manner, at the next opportunity. Or, if I am punished for a behavior immediately after engaging in the behavior, I will be far less likely to exhibit that behavior again. I will be inclined, at minimum, to avoid that behavior in the future.

Formative feedback, or behavior designed to alter the form or nature of the behavior, is most immediately useful *when it can be immediately applied.* When you step back and think about it for a minute, it is somewhat obvious that the most immediate opportunity to apply formative information is immediately *preceding* the next opportunity to engage in the behavior in question—not immediately *after* exhibiting the behavior.

Corrective information delivered immediately after exhibiting the behavior that cannot be immediately applied is generally taken as criticism, and criticism is punishing. Punishment reduces the probability of engaging in a behavior again at all if it can be avoided.

One of the most poignant examples of this I ever came across was in regard to a training program on Performance Improvement Counseling Sessions in a credit card center. There were a series of predictable quality and quantity problems in the processing of transactions in the center. A "needs assessment" had ascertained that even though the supervisors received timely and accurate data about these issues, there was very little coaching/counseling going on about these problems. When queried, the supervisors stated that they did not really feel all that comfortable in their coaching and counseling skills. Voilà, a classic training issue.

A performance-based training program was designed, utilizing actual performance data that the supervisors received each day. After being briefed on the outline and elements of a good coaching session, the training then turned to a series of practices with detailed feedback delivered to the trainees immediately after each practice. These practices were done in triads. The trainees would take turns performing one of three roles, playing the role of the supervisor doing the coaching, playing the worker receiving the coaching, and being an observer who provides feedback to the "supervisor" concerning how well they did in the practice. The trainees who had played supervisor in each practice were told precisely what they had done really well and precisely where they required further improvement. They would then shift roles for another practice round.

This last part of the training session allowed for each participant to play supervisor at least three times, and usually four times. After the last round was completed, they were given a two-sided "job aid" to replace the one they had been using in training. The new job aid had the outline for a performance improvement coaching session on the front (just like the one they used in practice) but now on the back they wrote down the most important areas where they had to improve on their coaching/counseling skills.

Ninety days later, an evaluation demonstrated that we had indeed impacted the frequency of counseling for work improvement. We had significantly less counseling going on than we had prior to the training. On investigation it came out that before the training intervention was done, most of the supervisors did not think they did counseling very well. After the training, the majority of the supervisors *knew* they did not do counseling very well, so they tried to avoid it.

Even though the supervisors were observably better at the process after the training than before the training, the fact of the matter was that while we had increased competence, we had at the same time diminished their confidence. Immediate formative feedback after each practice, coupled with the documentation of their weaknesses after their last practice had them focused on their weaknesses, not their strengths.

Corrective information provided immediately prior to a chance to use it is received as advice, and most people who are striving to improve their performance regard advice as positive and useful. The same information given immediately *after* the performance with no chance for immediate application is taken as criticism—which most people regard emotionally as punishing. Punishment is a form of motivational feedback that has the property of diminishing the probability of engaging in something again.

The difference between advice and punishment is simply a matter of timing. Feedback must be immediately useful and the timing for usefulness relates to the nature of the feedback. Motivational feedback should immediately follow the performance while formative feedback, or advice, should immediately precede the performance so that it can be immediately applied.

Specific. The feedback must not be ambiguous or generic. Telling someone that a 60-page report was a "good job" or that it was "okay but next time should be a bit better" with no detail about what or why it was good or not is hardly specific enough to be useful in either the motivational or formative form. It should be tied to the performance standards that we agreed on earlier.

Feedback on performance should include enough detail that there is no doubt in the mind of the person receiving it as to what they are being complimented on or being asked to improve.

Easy to Understand. The most common error here is around mixed messages in the feedback. Unfortunately there has been a lot of training about feedback that is frankly wrong—and one of the most common myths is the idea of "sandwiching" the feedback. The old saying of "tell them something good, then tell them what must change, and follow that by something good again" is a formula for misunderstanding. Just what *is* the message when you get both?

The best way to make feedback easy to understand is to keep the two forms of feedback separate—which lends itself nicely to getting the timing right anyway.

Usually efforts involved in making the person delivering the feedback feel more comfortable about giving it run counter to what is most useful and clear for the recipient of the feedback.

There is abundant research that says feedback on performance is critical to maintaining and improving performance. If you are unsure of how you are doing, it is quite hard to get better. As feedback is generally received from other parties (other than internal feedback against a performer's own standards), this area does not require a mental stretch to realize that checking this area of performance impact will require more than simply talking to the performer or watching the performance.

Skills and Knowledge

"At last," you may be tempted to say, "something that rests simply with the performer!" And you would be potentially more correct than not. However, even here there are potentially other issues interfering. The basic questions in this area include the following: Does the performer have the necessary skills and knowledge to perform? And does the performer know why the desired performance is important?

When you think systemically, even here there are potential ties that may require further investigation beyond the individual performer. If the performer does not have the requisite skills to perform to specification, and the performance in question is not a *new* requirement, resolving the problem permanently and ensuring it does not happen again with another performer, require asking and answering the following question. "If the individual does not have the required skills and knowledge, how and why did the person get into that position in the first place?" Researching and answering this question will take you places in the organization beyond the worker whose performance you are analyzing.

Further, if the performer doesn't know why the desired performance is important and you wish to rectify this situation in a manner that it does not happen again, you will be forced to take your Analysis elsewhere to institute a solution for both now and tomorrow with other similar workers. I cannot count the number of times that I have seen "performance" problems almost instantly resolved by the simple expedient of letting the workers know precisely *why* something has to be done in a particular way—which they often knew how to do, but simply did not think it mattered.

Individual Capacity

In terms of the traditional System variables relating to individual performance, this is the final area that must be investigated: "Is the performer physically, mentally, and emotionally able to perform?" Much like the questions above, if the answer is no, it raises other issues altogether about how and why the person is in the position in the first place. Once again, resolving this potential problem for future performers will require investigations and changes beyond the worker whose performance is being investigated.

Now, while this is the basic list of system variables when investigating and/or improving individual performance, it is hardly the end of the variables that must be considered when the performance under question occurs in a group setting. When the performance to be improved occurs in "public"—either while others watch and/or along with other performers doing the same individual tasks—or is performed by a group of people collectively as a team, every one of the variables listed so far are potentially altered with additional nuances that result from the group setting. In addition, there are a number of totally new additional variables that must be accounted for in the implementation of any given solution.

To make this point, here is a quick review of the "individual" system variables and how they are altered in a group setting.

Performance Standards/Specifications. Do others have different views or interpretations of the standards or specifications—particularly those viewed as "experts" in performing the task?

Performance Resources. Sufficient time and tools for one person or skill level may be insufficient for another person or skill level. This may make it hard to uncover deficiencies in this area. No one likes being the one requiring help when they perceive that there are others doing the same job who do not require the help.

Performance Support. A job aid that might be considered useful when operating alone can be considered demeaning or have some stigma attached to using it when performing in front of others.

Performance Interference. Inappropriate competition between performers can become an active interference with proper attention and focus on doing a proper job, as can the "social" expectations of fellow workers.

Performance Consequences. How a person feels they are being viewed by others who see them doing the task can be viewed by the performer as either positive or negative consequences. In the great majority of cases, people do care about how they are perceived.

Performance Feedback. Is the feedback given in public or in private? Either way can be either motivating or punishing, depending on the circumstances and how the performer getting feedback feels about the others who may be witnessing the feedback.

Skills and Knowledge. Appropriate skill or knowledge that is available may or may not be brought to bear while performing the job, depending on how the performer perceives the others who will view the performance. Most people do not want to be considered a dummy, nor do they wish to be considered a "show off" or "brown nose" or some sort of overachiever.

Individual Capacity. Similar to the comment immediately above, capacity can be hidden or fail to be applied if the social environment is not conducive to exhibiting the capacity. And then again there is the ubiquitous Peter Principle that does indeed run rife in organizational settings. Being steadily promoted until such time that you reach your level of incompetence, and then you stay there, is another variable that has to be investigated in terms of people being in positions for which they do not have the capacity to perform.

Additional systems variables that a group setting introduces include the following:

- Group norms, often referred to as a key piece of the organizational "culture."
  I can recall a classic example of group norms having a critical impact on what most would consider to be a simple and obvious example of working safely, yet the group norms totally twisted the issue. In a large distribution center in South Texas, we had an unacceptable rate of

hernias, and after running a series of classes, first voluntary and then mandatory, on lifting properly and utilizing the right equipment, the rate of hernias was unaffected and even appeared to be slowly increasing. A social research approach to the problem uncovered the issue of group norms.

It was a heavy and classic "macho" male culture in the warehouse. For whatever reason, the norm had developed that only a "wimp" took the time to "do things properly." Wearing the lifting belt labeled you as a pansy, as could lifting properly: "Any pansy can load a truck using a belt, but it takes a real man to simply grab that 50 gallon barrel and throw it onto the truck." The solution to the performance problem had nothing to do with skills and knowledge—it involved changing group norms and values that are an entirely different type of intervention than a straight skill and knowledge approach.

- Group think—or the ability of a group to see, or perceive, things that individuals alone will not. Or the fact that people in a group will think about things *differently* than any individual might have done on their own.

  A good example of this is the infamous phenomenon known as a "Trip to Abilene." This occurs in a group discussion when each person ends up, in the spirit of being a team player, deciding to do something primarily because he or she thinks the *others* want to do it and each individual does not want to be perceived as uncaring toward others or only thinking of him- or herself. The desire to be viewed as a "considerate" person or a team player overrides personal desires and opinions.

  This can result in a group taking an action that individually none of them would have chosen to take.

- Deference—the appropriate or inappropriate focus and attention given to "anointed" persons or functions in the immediate environment. A person can begin to have self-doubts when on his or her own he or she would have none and would have acted. But if a person who "everyone else" knows is the expert or power broker says or does something different, each individual may go along with that action and do or condone something that on his or her own would never have happened.

- Dominance—competitiveness between individual performers. The drive to win, be it overt or covert, can distort performance and cause individuals to lose sight of the actual objectives of the performance.

- Interdependence—tasks that cannot be performed by an individual alone has elements that are dependent on parts that others must perform. How this interdependence is handled can become a critical performance variable.

There is also a reasonably well researched set of variables that come to play in team settings and have a direct impact on the ability of any given team to work effectively, regardless of the task or tasks the team was charged with accomplishing.

When reviewing these "System" variables in relation to teams, keep in mind that the definition of a team, and the point at which these variables become relevant, is when there is a group of people who are in an interdependent relationship in regard to delivering some or all of the results expected from that group. There are 12 distinct variables that have an impact on the ability of a team to deliver the desired team results.

1. **The team does an effective job of sharing responsibility among its members**. No one wants to feel like they have to do more than their "fair" share.

2. **The team is willing to surface issues and deal constructively with conflicts that arise**. Discord and disagreements are not pushed under the table to fester.

3. **Team members tend to focus on constructive goals and aims rather than defending positions**. There is a general understanding that it is the "group" goal or goals that must take precedence over individual preferences and these must be related to internal and external value added.

4. **Team members are frank and open in expressing their ideas and concerns.** Everyone feels free to raise an issue or concern around the work and how it is done.

5. **The team is effective in eliciting the ideas of all its members.** Team members are not overlooked and views and suggestions are actually "solicited" (formally or informally) from everyone with regularity.

6. **The group stays focused on the tasks at hand.**

7. **Team members listen respectfully to each other.** The measure for this is that every team member will report that he or she is both heard and understood whenever he or she has anything to say.

8. **The team operates in a way that builds trust among its members.** Team members have to feel that their backs are covered, not spots of vulnerability.

9. **The team makes decisions through blending ideas rather than through force.** Team members do not feel pushed or forced into positions or actions. They feel a sense of camaraderie, not coercion.

10. **The team works together as a whole, rather than operating in cliques.** The team is indeed a team, not a conglomeration of diverse groups.

11. **The team values its members.** Team members feel valued by the others—they feel that their views, opinions, ideas, and feelings are sought out and valued by the rest of the team.

12. **In dealing with differences, team members spend at least as much time in trying to understand others' views as in persuading them of their own.** Consensus and understanding are more important than individually winning people over to "your" side. The strength of an individual's conviction is balanced with a desire to understand the views of others. Going forward as a group is more important than any individual prevailing in their views.

It is also true that for a team to be effective, there may be a requirement to have routine team meetings. This is not always the case, but when it is, when it is critical that the team get together to discuss team issues, there is yet another set of variables that come into play. These nine variables relate to effective team meetings:

1. Test progress and agreements frequently.

2. Value the opinions of all team members.

3. Ensure that the views of all members of the team are expressed and understood.

4. Attempt to build on each others' ideas; promote team collaboration over competition.

5. Demonstrate energy and enthusiasm during the meeting.

6. Effectively involve everyone in discussion so that a few people do not dominate.

7. Manage the time of the group effectively.

8. Demonstrate commitment to producing a high-quality result.

9. Work to set clear ground rules for working together.

And when you move from a simple group to groups of groups, or an organization, yet another list of variables are introduced that can have measurable impact on overall performance. Things like hierarchy, power, and cross functional perceptions/expectations all become potentially critical variables relating to performance in organizational settings. Policies, procedures, information systems, and structure—most of which are set or defined by people other than those actually doing any given piece of work—also become critical issues in the performance of both individuals and groups of individuals.

Hopefully the point has been made. Nothing in a System operates in isolation, not even the performance of an individual worker. The worker has an impact on people and things around him or her. The things and people around the worker in turn impact on the worker. And no matter how you may try to organize things, you cannot get away from this phenomenon and make the worker, or any given group of workers, independent of the System, nor the System independent of the worker or groups of workers. The point of all this in regard to Implementation of Performance Improvement projects is that all these variables must be considered and worked into the Implementation plan.

In the interest of time, a plan may be developed and put into place without a thorough System analysis—in fact, this is often the case. In most operations, speed is of the essence and the time and effort involved in a thorough System analysis for each and every performance issue are often not practical. This is not a problem and can save considerable time as long as the implementer has a good information/observation system in place to check for misalignment of any of these variables as the performance plan goes into effect.

A good mantra for an implementer is "analyze and plan for the obvious and known system variables, and have a good 'sensor' network in play to advise you if any of the other system variables begin to indicate a problem so that you can correct/ modify the plan as you go forward. It is well worth keeping in mind that the complexity of a solution to any given performance problem or opportunity will approach the complexity of the problem or opportunity, and as has been covered in the preceding pages, organizations are complex places.

At this point, it is probably worth turning this discussion around, however briefly, and view this whole system concept from the other direction. Think about a Human Performance Plan that is aimed at an entire organization or enterprise. The implementer must take into consideration and respond to all the levers discussed regarding individual performance, but consider them *within* the context of a work unit where the dynamics of the unit becomes an additional variable on individual performance and at the same time alters the characteristics/impact of some of the individual variables. Further, these unit dynamics are occurring *within* the context of groups of work units— where the dynamics of the overall group is affected by the various other units, and the other units are likewise affected by the overall group or organization. And finally, the organization dynamics operate *within* the context of a larger social system where the dynamics of the social system affect the organization, and the organization has an effect on the social system. None of these can be separated out—it is in the end *one* whole System. The European Union has made more formal strides in recognizing this aspect of System than has been done in North America. The concept of formal statements and plans reflecting this awareness is becoming institutionalized in the form of published CSRs. Published and formalized statements of Corporate Social Responsibility in which organizations attempt to recognize, identify, and acknowledge their impact on society and the environment and thereby drive this awareness throughout the organization and reflect it in their strategic plans and tactical actions throughout the organization.

Another comment on system and organizational performances has to be made here. With little exception, it takes group-based techniques to successfully analyze and have an impact on group-based performance. Individual-based applications of HPT, such as e-learning, are generally less effective and efficient when dealing with group-based performance.

In the interest of cost savings and being more "state of the art" and high tech, a good many ill-conceived implementations have been attempted with e-learning and various other "individual"-based techniques around what are essentially group-based phenomena.

There are also many attempts to perfect or maximize the performance of isolated or individual groups or units, which is equally ill-conceived and inappropriate.

To be truly effective managing anything within a System, you have to be sensitive to the entire System. Within a System, it is a "zero-sum" game: if any part of the System becomes "too weak" or "too strong," the entire system is diminished in effectiveness.

The point being made in this chapter is that human performance, be it that of an individual, an entire enterprise, or anything in between, occurs within a System. And in reality, it is "one System," and a quite large one at that. Attempting to treat it as anything less is playing the part of the venerable ostrich and sticking your head in the sand. If you limit your view sufficiently, you can convince yourself that all is right with your plan. An often heard cry when discussing System and Performance Improvement plans is that this is too hard, too demanding, too complex, and, at minimum, very inconvenient. All of these complaints about system are at one level absolutely true, but this also brings to mind the "error" of Cardinal Bellarmine and Pope Urban VIII in 1624. At that time, it is was certainly politically and socially troublesome and inconvenient for Galileo to state that the earth moved around the sun and not vice versa, and it was therefore declared to be in error. However, it did not change the reality any. This was finally corrected by the Catholic Church in 1893, and in 1979, Pope John Paul II apologized to Galileo. Hopefully it will not take as long for the Human Performance community to come to grips with the reality of the System situation. It may not be convenient, but it is the reality, and if you want to impact performance, especially at the organizational level, with any long-term impact, it is a reality that must be incorporated into performance plans and interventions.

And finally to close this chapter on System, it is important to note that effective systems are by definition about overall balance. And the concept of balance brings us into the topic of Alignment—which is the next chapter.

Endnote

1. System thinking and planning is covered extensively in the first book in this series, Kaufman (2006). *Change, Choices, and Consequences.*

Chapter 2
Alignment

In the previous chapter, the importance of understanding that all organizations are a System, or even more properly, subsystems within a larger societal System, was provided. As was discussed in the previous chapter, lasting attempts to improve the performance of any System or subsystem must be done within the context of the overall System. To do otherwise would be as if exercising one's legs was enough to provide full fitness and health. While easy to say, it is considerably less easy to accomplish. What helps is a practical tool or model to guide diagnosis, design, and implementation of Performance Improvement efforts. The multiple threads of the System can get incredibly difficult to keep in mind. A good model is scalable—applicable at whatever size System or subsystem targeted for a performance intervention.

This chapter covers the Organizational Alignment Model. This model is both sufficiently simple to enable the nonspecialist to understand and use and still have the depth and robustness to serve the System specialist in their activities.

While the alignment model *could* be applied to an individual performer working in isolation with no interactions or dependencies with anyone else, that is one level of system where this model would add very little in terms of utility. The issues of system applied at the individual level are relatively straightforward, and an overriding or organizing tool such as the Organizational Alignment Model is not necessary (but might be useful to ensure that what is done and delivered adds value within and outside the organization). While the principles still apply, the model does not add much to understanding and planning beyond what is already covered in the discussion of performance at the individual level that was discussed in the previous chapter.

ORGANIZATIONAL ALIGNMENT MODEL

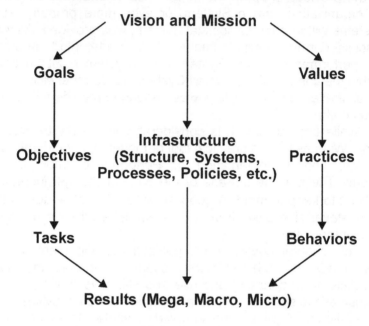

External Environment - Societal Value Added (Mega)

Vision and Mission

Goals   Values

Objectives   Infrastructure   Practices
(Structure, Systems,
Processes, Policies, etc.)

Tasks   Behaviors

Results (Mega, Macro, Micro)

Stakeholders

Based on © Vanguard Consulting and Vector Group Inc. 1987, 2005

However, once you put the individual performer into even a very small group of individuals that, however minimally, must coordinate their efforts to deliver the expected results, the utility of this model is quite large. As the System gets larger, the variables that must be tracked and coordinated begin to multiply and some form of organizing tool becomes extremely valuable. And from team performance through organizational systems composed of multiple groups or complete enterprises, the potential complexity increases geometrically. At these higher levels of complexity, it is highly useful and arguably critical to have a good organizing model for guiding and balancing performance diagnostics and interventions.

Vision and Mission[1]

Groups exist within an external environment. From the performance analyst perspective, when the group is a team or function within a larger organization, the larger organization can be considered the "external environment" within which the group operates. While the term "external environment" is usually reserved for communities and society when you are working on performance characteristics of a small team within a much larger organization (such as a 12-person accounting audit function within a 25,000 person manufacturing organization), trying to take the Analysis and Design all the way to the classic external environment has dubious value.

However, if the performance target is a large multi-group organization or entire enterprise, the external environment must be the larger society—the Mega level—within which the organization operates, including things such as customers, suppliers/ vendors, competition, regulatory bodies, the community, the environment and society as a whole and its collective future. The external environment is all the things outside of the target group, but that have an impact on the target group, and must be given due consideration within the performance plan if maximum impact and performance is to be expected. While the external environment is often loosely or only partially defined, and often difficult to specify in terms of an enterprise, it is relatively easy to access and quantify when dealing with an individual, group, or function within an organization.

The model shows that in direct response to the "external environment" is the vision and mission of the working group. Vision statements and mission statements are not the same— even though many organizations confuse them. A *mission* is a statement of what the organization has been created to deliver, its reason for existence, and should include measurable criteria related to the vision—the value added to external clients and society. A *vision* is a statement of what must be delivered to external clients and our shared society and *could* be achieved and/or the possible result of exemplary achievement of the mission.

For the purposes of Alignment and more specifically for Implementation of performance plans, which is what this discussion is about, the importance of the difference between a mission statement and a vision statement is nominal if and only if what gets delivered outside of the organization adds measurable value to external clients. Either way, the vision statement and related mission statement are about the "intent" of the organization and the reason for existing at all.

When it comes to implementing Performance Improvement plans, it is nothing less than astonishing how often it turns out that there was lack of clarity, focus, or agreement on the purpose of the group and how the performance plan does or does not reflect that purpose. In my own experience, I have found this "lack of clarity or focus" to be more pronounced as you move up the organizational hierarchy and organizational levels—until you reach the Chief Executive Officer. At the bottom levels of most organizations, there is often a reasonably clear and balanced view of what should be happening. As you move up the organization, the focus often gets more and more blinkered and becomes more and more functionally focused. The common term I hear is "silos" in the organization that are so focused on their own piece of the organization that they lose sight of the systemic quality of all organizations. All functions and all levels should ground themselves firmly in the overall vision and mission of the organization and develop vision and mission statements for their area(s) of responsibility that reflect its connection, clearly and unambiguously, to the total system and its purpose for life.

Three Directional Forces

Continuing on through the model from this statement of overall intent or purpose, there are three sources of guidance concerning what is appropriate and/or inappropriate in the pursuit of this purpose. The primary guidance for appropriate *tasks* is represented on the left side of the model. Primary guidance on appropriate *behavior* is represented on the right side of the model.

In the middle of the model, we have a basket of things that the organization provides to support and/or control the group as it pursues the accomplishment of its purpose. These infrastructure elements also provide guidance, either overtly or by implication, regarding what is appropriate and/or inappropriate in the pursuit of the group's intent. The right-hand and left-hand paths along their vertical columns provide increasing detail from concept at the top to tasks and behaviors at the bottom of each column.

The Tactical Path

The left-hand column of the Alignment model is often referred to as the tactical path to results, or *what* the group is supposed to be doing to deliver results. This column starts with broad goals, that are then translated into measurable objectives, that in turn are translated into specific tasks and activities intended to achieve the objectives.

This tactical path of increasing detail as to what is expected is one of the oldest known methods of providing guidance to an organization. For many years, it was considered one of the primary activities, if not *the* primary activity, of managing an organization to deliver consistent, desired, and useful results.

The concept of "cascading" this clarity down through the organization, unit by unit with increasing detail, was developed and refined and, by the 1950s, was generally considered to be the primary manner of providing focus and clarity to ensure that the organization as a whole achieved its overall intent.

Many of the management gurus of the time felt that the dominance of some companies in their relative industry was totally, or at least partially, due to the effectiveness of their abilities to ensure this cascade of strategic clarity, from the total overall organization on down through divisions, functions, and departments to the smallest working unit.

The Cultural Path

Starting in the 1960s and growing on through the 1970s, there came a realization that there was more to exemplary organizational performance than just clarity on the strategy, tactics, and tasks related to achieving the mission and vision. The right hand of the model represents this later realization that behaviors were also a critical element in organizational effectiveness—particularly when derived from and tied to the vision and mission statements of the organization. The right-hand side of the model is often referred to as the *cultural* path to results. Issues such as quality, service, and innovation when investigated seemed to relate more to behavioral issues than the actual tasks being performed. Things like attitude, demeanor, and values came to the forefront as equally important aspects of organizational direction and results. The criticality of *how* the people in the group or organization went about performing their tasks became clear. Further, it became clear that behavioral guidance, unlike task guidance, was more related to what was observed than what was written down.

The behavioral patterns and expectations of the members of the organization provide guidance as to *how* things are supposed to be done, or the "manner and demeanor" that is appropriate while engaging in organizational tasks. This organizational culture may be overtly or covertly defined, but it exists either way and sets standards for acceptable and nonacceptable behaviors and actions. In many ways, you could say the organizational culture is the embodiment of the rules of the "social network" that surrounds the people while they are doing the work of the organization. Another definition of corporate culture is "how we do things around here."

Like the tactical side of the model, this side also has a progression from overarching principles or values down through practices (measurable statements of behavioral intent) to daily behaviors and required performance. Just like the tactical side where there are often a variety of ways to achieve the objectives, on the cultural side there are a variety of behaviors that can equally achieve the behavioral and resulting performance intent that is embodied in the practices.

In a financial services organization, for example, there was a vision statement about being the country's best provider of personal financial advice and solutions. This vision was a long way from reality and lacked specificity and did not deal with external clients and societal value added. Since the "vision" was such a stretch, they made sure the mission statement provided more direct and immediate guidance on how to get to the "vision." Part of this mission statement included "improving our cost/income ratio from the current £2.82 of cost per £1.00 of income (yes, they were losing considerable amounts of money) to a target of £1.00 cost per £2.00 revenue booked within three years. Achieving this rather large shift in results would require all people and units in the organization to collaborate heavily as the processes involved in the cost/income ratio ran through all areas of the organization. This gave rise to an organizational value of "working together—as success comes through effective collaboration"—a value statement based on the vision/ mission, or at least the pathways to those.

A value statement this broad is difficult to measure and is usually first stated in fuzzy and process terms. More specificity is helpful in guiding people as they go about their work each day. This value was broken down into four practices:

- Promoting a team culture

- Creating an environment where people share views, expertise, and best practice

- Working with those holding different views in a constructive manner

- Working to achieve common goals and beat the competition

Each of the above practices is specific enough that they can be incorporated into a 360° feedback instrument that will allow relevant constituencies to rate any particular individual's behavior on each practice utilizing a Likert scale of 1 to 7 where 1 is "never behaves this way" and 7 is "always behaves this way," thereby quantifying the adherence to the stated practice.

360° Feedback

When looking at the topic of 360° feedback, you have a tactic with huge potential for Performance Improvement. At the same time, this is a topic that, *as currently applied in most organizations*, has little to no impact on overall organizational performance.

360° feedback has become quite popular over the past 20 years. There are many commercial surveys available that are marketed quite heavily. In spite of all this, I have to state that in my own experience, which is reasonably extensive, I have yet to find an off-the-shelf 360° instrument that was useful and effective in furthering organizational performance.

There are a few off-the-shelf surveys that are not bad for use in generalized "management development." But management development is not organizational development and the connection between organizational performance and management development is quite weak at best.

Management development is focused on a set of generalized management competencies that are broadly applicable in any organization on any given management assignment. Organizational performance is about the organization delivering on its strategic intent. These two purposes are not necessarily aligned.

When focusing on management development, the focus is on the individual and his or her ability to handle management positions *in general.* Often there are courses (and occasionally 360° instruments) that are focused on the particular skill sets utilized in a particular level of management—i.e., supervisory, middle management, and executive. However, the skill sets are still generic and intended to be broadly applicable across a range of positions in any organization. By definition, in an off-the-shelf survey instrument, there is nothing in the survey that is specific to the individual organization utilizing that instrument.

There are a few instruments that allow some degree of limited "customization" by allowing the using organization to add up to 10 questions to the overall survey. While this is a marginal improvement, it is still only marginal. Also, if you think about the logic of this approach, how many organizations are there that can define the critical elements in their competitive edge via 10 survey questions? And while this minor addition of a few items might be a marginal improvement in the relevance of topics surveyed it still does not address the other significant problems with off-the-shelf packages.

A second problem with off-the-shelf instruments is in regard to the language and overall management model utilized. People filling out the survey have to understand the language being used, the "operational definitions" of the terms used in the survey instrument, and how they correlate (if at all) with the way those words and concepts are used in any one particular organization. This problem relates to not only the people filling out the instrument, but also with the managers getting the feedback.

The most effective and accurate survey instrument will use words, terms, and phrases that are in alignment with the way those things are discussed and talked about in the organization where the survey is being utilized. And if you are focusing on the development and maintenance of competitive edge it has to focus on those aspects of the overall organizational value proposition that are deemed to be competitive. These issues vary organization by organization.

A 360° feedback instrument that is intended to aid in the advancement of *organizational* performance will not be focused on *generic* management competencies. If the intent is to improve organizational performance, the instrument must focus on the particular management practices that are central to the organizational strategy and the development and maintenance of competitive edge.

Competitive edge is not established by focusing on generic skill levels. An off-the-shelf 360° feedback instrument will do no more than ensure that an organization's management is no worse than that of their competitors in the application of general management principles.

Another rather large problem with generic 360° feedback is that no actual management or supervisory job is generic in practice. Each and every workgroup is somewhat unique, and the appropriate balance and focus of management and leadership skills that best fit the situation will vary management position by management position. And further, even within any given management position, the appropriate mix of management skills will vary as the make-up of the subordinate or peer group varies over time.

Let me give one simple and actual example to highlight what I mean: When I was doing a project for one of the national labs, I was struck by the organizational structure that strongly pointed out this "uniqueness of each supervisory job" phenomenon. In the division in which I was working there were two kinds of work groups—research groups and technical support groups.

Each group was composed of 6 to 12 employees and a supervisor. A typical research group would be made up of the supervisor plus 6 to 12 Ph.D.s. The staff had an average tenure of 15+ years on the job and may have included a Nobel laureate or two. A typical technical support group was composed of a supervisor and 6 to 12 people who on average had a two-year or undergraduate degree (possibly one or two with a Master's degree) and averaged 2 to 4 years on the job.

Supervisors engaged in job rotation in that lab and could easily shift between a research group one year and a support group the next. Regardless of which type of group you were supervising, the job was one of "first line supervision." But is it reasonable to assume that the exact same set of supervisory skills were most appropriate regardless of which group you were supervising?

I will contend that the answer is rather obvious—the exact same pattern of supervisory skills *would not be* appropriate. The groups, while both were considered front line, were considerably different, both in the tasks in which they engaged as well as in the skills and knowledge of the staff.

While there are indeed an identifiable set of generic skills of front line supervision, these generic skills are not applied equally in all situations. In fact, each situation is different and the relative balance and focus of required supervisory skills will vary as a function of the knowledge, expertise, and activity of each workgroup.

Working on generic skills can help a manager or supervisor generally improve his or her broad-based management knowledge. However, working on generic skills will rarely result in specific and strategically relevant group improvement in any given organizational setting. Improvement in group performance requires a focus on the skills and knowledge most relevant to that particular work unit at that particular point in time.

Another problem with 360° surveys is that the higher the management level, the less impact a basic 360° survey will have. Data from a 360° survey, particularly subordinate data, can be quite powerful at the first line supervision level and up into the middle management levels. Additionally, as you move into middle management, the peer data generated by a 360° survey can also be quite useful and powerful. However, by the time you get to the executive level, a standard 360° survey begins to lose most of its potential impact.

In the lower levels of management and supervision, the manager is usually experiencing sets of similar issues and is repeatedly dealing with these issues. The manager will tend to look on activities like "giving assignments" or "counseling for work improvement" as routine and repetitive issues. At senior levels, there is a distinct tendency to view each of these types of issues on an individual basis, focusing on the unique aspects of each and every occurrence. Feedback data from a 360° survey does not reflect this type of outlook, and as such, more senior managers will view 360° feedback as simplistic and superficial. As you move into senior levels of management, more customized and individualized data is required to have the same power and relevance from the executive's perspective. The Management Mirror is a far more impactful process for providing effectiveness feedback to senior levels of management. This process is discussed in more depth in Chapter 6.

One last major problem with traditional 360° feedback has to do with the way the surveys are usually analyzed and reported back to the subject managers. With only one exception that I know of, these types of survey data are fed back to managers in a standardized "percentile" format. As the subject manager, you will see how you rank when compared to some larger database of managers. For example, on each question you will know that X% of typical managers will score higher on that question and Y% will score lower on that question. This process of feeding back standardized percentile scores to managers has three major problems with it:

1. Managers who find that they are in the top 15% on any particular question have a tendency to assume they are "just fine" on that item and don't have to really think about it. This may or may not be true:

   a) The manager may be spending time doing something that, while he or she does it well, is not necessary to do for their particular group.

   b) The manager may be able to garner *even greater* results with increased emphasis on something he or she already does well.

   c) Any level of performance can be improved on. Even Olympic gold medal athletes continue to practice and improve.

2. Managers who find that they are in the bottom 20% on any particular question have a tendency to "give up" on that particular point. The "gap" is just too great to try to overcome.

3. When the manager is being compared to other managers and the scores are not outstanding, it leads to a strong tendency to NOT share the data with other managers or staff. It makes you look bad and that is hard for the average manager to freely embrace. Further, if your data are truly outstanding, there is a tendency to avoid openly discussing the data because it can look like you are bragging or "blowing your own horn."

   This phenomenon runs in direct opposition to one of the most powerful development and change opportunities for managers when reviewing 360° feedback. The greatest force for change and improvement comes when managers and supervisors discuss their results with their peers and their subordinates. The truth of the matter is that you cannot fully understand the feedback you get from a 360° without open dialogue with the people who filled it out. And the best ideas for improvement often come from open discussion with peers when you are comparing results with each other and discussing why you got scored the way you did and what you might do about it.

The answer to all three of these issues is to utilize ipsative feedback rather then percentile feedback. Ipsative data do not allow for comparisons between individuals. The data are reported in a manner that only lets you know your personal relative strengths and weaknesses across your personal data set. The manager's individual scores are averaged across their entire data set, and then the personal results are reported as a standard deviation from the individual average. What the manager does the most or best and what she or he does the least or worst is identified, but only in comparison to how that manager does on the other practices surveyed.

When the data are presented this way, around a manager's own personal average, everyone getting feedback has both ups and downs. Everyone will have as many pluses as minuses. The individual manager will also receive data on his or her percentile rating, but that will be on a separate form and kept private. The feedback display that is used for discussions with peers, the boss, subordinates, and others will not show that data. It will show the relative strong points and weak points, but they will be relative only in regard to that particular manager. In this approach, everyone will have strengths to leverage and everyone will have issues to improve on.

There is no question that 360° feedback can be a highly useful and powerful tactic to apply in pursuit of improved organizational performance. This is particularly true in regard to the always critical aspect of how effective leadership and management practices are applied in support of the organizational strategy. To be effective, however, the survey must be totally customized, focusing on the particular and unique characteristics that will differentiate the organization from its competitors.

It must also reflect the language and terms that are in normal use in the subject organization. The survey form must be designed based on data that come from a good organizational diagnostic such as the organizational scan. Off-the-shelf 360° feedback forms have no functional place in organizational performance interventions.

360° Feedback and Cloning

It should also be obvious that there are numerous potential behaviors that could be utilized to achieve any given practice. Consider the following practice: promoting a team culture. There are numerous behaviors a person could exhibit that would promote a team culture. The choice of what behaviors to utilize could be left to personal style and team context. However, these statements, while well-intentioned, focus on means and assume the ends. More clarity of what performance is required must be added to value statements such as these.

One of the concerns I have often heard about 360° feedback, or culture change programs for that matter, is that the process is designed to make everyone behave the same and reduce or eliminate individuality. I have heard the statement "this process is an attempt to turn out people who are 'cookie cutter' clones all marching in mindless 'lock step'." This is most pointedly not true with surveys that are focused on supervisory/ management *practices* rather than specifically detailed behaviors or processes. Focusing on practices leaves plenty of room for customization of behaviors and personal style—yet at the same time there is enough specificity to exclude many dysfunctional behaviors and provide guidance on appropriate ways of behaving. As is embodied in the first of the performance professional standards, the focus is on *results*.

360° Feedback and Likert Items and Scales

Feedback from a 360° survey and similar surveys is dependent on the proper utilization of Likert items and Likert scales. A Likert item is a survey question that asks the respondent to indicate his or her degree of agreement or disagreement with the item statement along some scale indicating degree of agreement/disagreement.

Please circle the appropriate number:

The manager supports my efforts.

Never 1 2 3 4 5 6 7 Always

A very common error that diminishes the usefulness of data of this type can be tied to a misunderstanding of Likert's research. Many people seem to incorrectly assume that a Likert item has a 5-point scale. What Likert actually said is that for items of this type to have the granularity to be maximally useful, the bulk of the responses must be spread across at least 5 points on the scale.

When you are querying people on the behavior of others, most people will avoid the two extremes represented by each end of the scale. Choices like "never" and "always" are a bit too extreme for most people to check but none the less are appropriate anchors for giving meaning to a scale. What this means is that when you only have 5 points on the scale, you will have most of your data, often all of it, spread across only three points. A 7-point response space (as above) allows the ends to be avoided and still have the data spread across 5 points that gives far more granularity in terms of agreement or disagreement and allows for significantly more sensitivity in understanding "degree" of agreement or disagreement. This subtlety can make a huge difference in the quality and focus or action plans resulting from feedback of this type.

Cookbooks versus Guidelines

The place many performance specialists go wrong with performance plans, particularly when dealing with culture or management topics, is to approach the performance issues in an algorithmic manner or as a cookbook. The reality of many aspects of organizational performance, and especially issues like management and culture, is that they are best understood in a heuristic manner. It is about general principles and guidelines, not a specific formula. It is about providing sufficient detail on the *results* (and the value these results will add to delivering on the mission and vision) that are expected such that people can ascertain if what they are doing is appropriate, without limiting the ability to bring their own style and choices into the solution. Once there is agreement on the results, each individual can decide how he or she, working with others, will get those results. First measurably define the required results and then let people decide how to get there.

This kind of guideline is called a *heuristic,* and in general, heuristics are far more relevant and usable over cookbooks (also called algorithms) when dealing with organizational issues as well as when dealing with leadership and management issues generally.

A heuristic provides aid or direction in the solution of a problem, but does not specify a solution. It may provide indicators of a solution, but not a straight, unvarying path. A heuristic leaves open the possibility of multiple paths to a solution or performance enhancement—there is not just *one* way to deliver the desired result.[2]

Over-Specification

Far too many performance plans focus on a particular formula and are way too limiting in their guidance generally focusing on one given particular instance with specific behaviors or actions to apply. In effect, the entire process for a given specific situation will be detailed—a "cookbook" approach—and the focus is on the steps in the process, point by point.

A focus on the desired result and how it will be recognized or measured is a characteristic of a heuristic, with indicators or suggestions as to "ways" to achieve the result. Management in general is primarily a heuristic, as are most solutions to group and organizational performance. This is particularly true with cultural issues of organizational performance. It is well worth it for the performance specialist to keep in mind, that overall business is far more a heuristic world than one driven by cookbooks. Peter Drucker (1973) notes that it is more important to do what is right rather than just doing things right.

To be most effective, both the tactical path and cultural path to results must be firmly grounded in the organizational mission and vision statements. If anything, the cultural path is arguably even more important to have clear and unambiguous ties to the business of the organization—what business is it of the organization to attempt to direct people's personal behavior or management style unless they are restrictions on ethics and lawful behavior? The considerable work on quality management supports this: people know best how to do their jobs once they agree on the quality of what is to be produced.[3]

Infrastructure

The middle of the alignment model, labeled "Infrastructure," is a collection of policies, procedures, systems, and information flows that are also intended to support and/or guide daily behavior (which will lead to the achievement of the mission and the vision). Unlike the more formal tactical and cultural paths, this body of organizational artifacts is often, on the surface, unrelated to the vision and mission statements. These are things that are usually created by various staff groups in the organization in response to some specific governance, regulatory, or specific staff functional requirement—many of them driven by the finance and legal departments—and often responding to a perceived internal problem or external requirement or regulation. However, even though many, if not most, of these artifacts are not formally considered part of the tactical guidelines for the organization, they can, and often do, have significant measurable impact on the effectiveness of the organization. Anything that facilitates or limits actions on a routine, regular, and often daily basis *is* a message from the organization that, in the mind of the employee, reflects what the organization is about.[4]

Messages that are sent and received routinely are obviously important and must represent key issues for the organization. When you think about it, it is often the case that these possibly unintended messages about purpose and desired activity will outweigh in sheer quantity the more intended messages that come down the tactical path. Informal messages are very much a part of an organization's culture. They are often sent without the sender realizing it.

Infrastructure issues are often overlooked when dealing with business results, particularly when they at first glance do not seem to have any relationship to the issues at hand, but this can be a huge mistake. You have to investigate carefully the entire system, as I covered in the previous chapter, and that includes this area of infrastructure.

Here is an example:

The client was a computer services division that comprised over 3,000 people operating out of offices across the country. This division provided service to clients all across the country, looking after their mainframe, micro, mini, and desktop computers and all the related peripheral gear.

The 3,000 managers and staff of the division were domiciled in more than 40 zone offices scattered across the country, from which engineers and technicians were dispatched to serve the customers in their zone.

At that point in time, there were 13 firms in the country providing a similar service nationally. The magazines *Computer Weekly* and *Data Pro Magazine* began doing a yearly survey of users of services of this type and provided a league table each year in terms of customer satisfaction. The client had just received a copy of the first survey, and it was ranked 13th of the 13 providers.

The rankings varied slightly by zone, but only slightly, and coming in 10th rather than 13th in some better zones was not something in which to find any solace. It was clearly not a localized problem. It should come as no surprise that this did not exactly fit the company's strategic planning objectives and they figured they had a serious organizational performance problem.

A detailed diagnostic uncovered some significant problems all right, but not where they expected to find them. As is often the case in situations of broad-based service failure, the problems, while pervasive, did not reside with the technicians and engineers who actually called on the customers and provided the service. The answers lay elsewhere in the organizational system. There was one particularly notable piece that rested squarely within the infrastructure part of the alignment model—notable in relation to the problem, not that it simply jumped out at the person doing the analysis. It was a subtle relationship that did not surface from a detailed review of services delivered, nor from a casual look at the overall System.

Each of the engineers and technicians were assigned a specific vehicle—a car or van—that was their personal transportation to and from the client work sites. The engineer or technician had personal responsibility for ensuring that the vehicle (especially a van) was stocked with an appropriate mix of computer parts and related gear. In addition, while all expenses were paid directly by the company, they had personal responsibility for ensuring that the car's or van's general maintenance schedule was followed.

The division had a fleet of over 2,000 vehicles, which represented a significant investment on the part of the company. Roughly every three years, each technician or engineer would turn in his or her vehicle and get a new one. The company would sell the used vehicles and recoup part of the capital invested in the fleet.

The finance department of the company, doing its proper task of overseeing major capital outlays, had done an analysis of the resale values the company was getting on average as this fleet turned over every three years. The analysis showed that due to poor adherence to maintenance procedures, they were getting roughly 70% of the value they *should* have gotten if the vehicles had been better maintained.

Auditing and overseeing the vehicle maintenance records were part of the management responsibility of all zone managers but it clearly was not happening with any reliability. Literally millions of pounds sterling were being lost as a result of poor maintenance.

This was clearly a breach of company policy as well as a significant drain on the limited capital resources of the company. Zone management was failing in its assigned responsibilities. Two rounds of increasingly terse "reminders" from the CFO to zone and division management did not resolve the problem. The finance department then, quite justifiably from its perspective, went to the last resort and made this item a "top priority" (and therefore mandatory) checkpoint on the internal audit review that each and every office went through yearly. Any failure on a "priority" item would have significant consequences for the zone manager in his or her yearly personal performance review.

This action did alleviate the vehicle resale value problem.

Now let's return to the zone office and the customer service problem. As stated earlier, the engineers and technicians were dispatched from the zone office to the various customer sites where the work was performed. This meant that if the office was being productive, the engineers and technicians spent very little time in the office, and therefore their time with their supervisor was equally limited.

The daily schedule for the typical office was that the staff would arrive in the morning and the first thing to occur was the parceling out of assignments to the field staff to get them "off and running" as quickly as possible. Then at the end of the day, as the field staff returned to the office to park their cars and vans, there would be a brief period of interaction with their supervisor again to report on the day, after which they would get into their own private vehicles and go home.

Since the vehicle maintenance activity became a "priority item" on the internal audit checklist, the total time available for each supervisor interaction had become solely focused on vehicle maintenance and parts inventory (an item that had gone onto the priority audit review a few years earlier). There was literally no time to even discuss customers and the day's activity. All end-of-day discussion with the supervisor was about car maintenance and parts inventory. The engineer or technician would come back to the office after a day of servicing customers, and from their perspective, the only thing the supervisor "wanted" to talk about was vehicles and parts and their cost to the company.

Over the following year what was the message to the engineers and technicians as to the company focus and interest—service or control of company assets?

The engineers and technicians, from their perspective, had a clear view of the real agenda in the company. Not only were the company assets—vehicles and parts—the only "real" focus for the organization, it was so pervasive that staff even made sure they left the customer site in time to meet with their supervisor to have this discussion before going home, even if it meant not completing the service call.

From the employee perspective, these infrastructure elements are some of the most pervasive indicators of the organization's "real" agendas and often result in more "real" or functional overall guidance in terms of organizational values and priorities than anything else in the organization.

To be fair and to complete the picture, there were monthly zone meetings with all hands in attendance during which the company strategy was reviewed, and service was clearly emphasized by the zone manager. But, with the daily behavior so clear, these monthly meetings became points of additional dissatisfaction for the service staff, and points of "proof" that management only gave required lip service to customer satisfaction. Instead of enhancing the focus on customers, the monthly meeting became a source of increasing distrust and dissatisfaction with management who from the staff perspective would *say* one thing at the required monthly zone meetings but would actually *do* something completely different when it came to daily management.

Best Intentions and Villains

Please keep in mind that in this case, there actually were no villains anywhere. Everyone, the finance department included, was doing the best they could to fulfill the responsibilities of their respective jobs. But nonetheless, the System got out of alignment with the overall strategy and purpose of the company. The infrastructure piece was not systemically grounded in the strategy with pieces of it reflecting only particular subsystems.

The importance of the infrastructure piece, in terms of consequences to the managers, became overbearing and more critical in real terms than the business strategy, their competitive position, or the creation of a service-oriented culture.

The Reality of Organizational Direction Setting

When people, or a group of people, go to work, they get *direction* from all three paths indicated in the alignment model on page 40. There is a job assignment, often with multiple tasks, that a person or group is assigned to accomplish. This is coupled with observations of the people with whom they work and the supervisory/management behaviors being exhibited in relation to the work and people. And finally, the information, tools, processes, and procedures that must be utilized or adhered to while at work also give indications of what is important and what is not.

All three of these forces—the business plan (based on strategy and the vision and mission), which includes "the plan for today"; the behavioral (performance) norms that are being exhibited all around the "worker" (or the culture); and the types of tools, information, tracking, procedures, and policies that the organization requires, makes available, or doesn't make available—provide ongoing real-time guidance as to what is expected from the employees of the organization.

Alignment is about getting all three of these "directional forces" pointing in the same direction and delivering compatible messages that are supportive of each other. Lack of Alignment leads to uncertainty, lack of action, and general nonresponsiveness to one or more aspects of the organizational business intent.

These three forces of organizational direction are what lead to the middle path, which is the critical piece for the performance profession. In the end, it is the Results delivered to the organizational stakeholders that we must be concerned with, not individual sub-pieces. It is all one System that must be aligned. It has to all come together cohesively for the Results to show maximal valued returns to organizational stakeholders. As performance improvement specialists, it is the overall Results on which we must focus.

When it comes to Implementation of Performance Improvement plans, be they individual, team, function, or enterprise, the critical and relevant aspects of the Alignment model are the vision/mission of the group within which the performance plan is being implemented and the alignment of the three directional forces indicated in the model to deliver the overall result(s) required by the enterprise.

When these directional forces are out of alignment, or even *perceived* to be pointing in different directions, clarity of organizational intent becomes cloudy, and variance in performance increases. Confusion in regard to organizational direction/purpose leads to people having to spend increased amounts of energy and effort to figure out priorities, what to do, and how to do it, and this increased effort is, by necessity, focused internally rather than externally on customers and/or the competition. At one level, this is a simple equation: As the internal effort and energy required to get things done goes up, there is less and less time and energy available to focus on customers and competition, diminishing the quantity, and potentially the quality, of the results delivered.

There are those in the performance business, including this author, who will contend that at the organizational/enterprise level, managing performance is *all* about Alignment. Management of Alignment and management of organizational performance are synonymous.

Organizational Alignment is about maximizing organizational effectiveness—meeting the mission—and overall organizational performance by elimination of conflicting and/or confusing messages from the three primary sources of direction.

But, what about performance improvement plans focused on divisions, departments, functions, work units, or individual performers? How critical is this alignment notion when dealing with less than an entire enterprise? Potentially, it is quite critical regardless of the size of the entity targeted for performance improvement. The larger the entity, the more absolute the criticality becomes. The more people there are involved in accomplishing the targeted task(s), the more important it is for there to be cohesive Alignment.

The logic here is inescapable. If there are multiple people involved in getting any particular result and there are divergent views about priorities or what and how things are to be done, problems arise. The probability of interfering with each other, conflict between people and groups, and disorder in general goes up—which means results go down.

The best way to make this point is probably to go directly to the lowest level of performance improvement plans—the individual level—and look at the issue of misalignment at this most basic level.

At the individual level, a performance plan should be checked against the Alignment of the group within which the individual works. If the details of Alignment are not known at the group level, there is a strong requirement to work that void—it will enhance the probability of the individual performance plan working. Of course the same is true all the way up the organizational levels, but it is most poignant at the individual level.

Remember, each and every day, as each individual comes to work, he or she is receiving guidance, both overtly and covertly, from all three directional forces of the alignment model. This is a pervasive input—none of these three can be "put on hold." They simply happen, either by conscious plan or covertly by implication.

Imagine the content of a specific performance plan aimed at a specific individual. Now imagine that the plan, or some elements of the plan, *appears* to the individual to be in conflict with what other people around them are doing. What if the supervisor or supervisor's supervisor seems more interested in something else or even simply disinterested in some or all elements of the performance plan? What if elements of the infrastructure (policies, procedures, budgets, job descriptions, available tools/information/time, etc.) appear to impede or interfere with the ability of the person to implement the performance plan? Any of these factors will lead to a diversion of focus and a diminishing of perceived importance in regard to the performance plan or elements of the performance plan. Further, the individual will have to make judgments on what and how to proceed where there is perceived conflict or differences in priorities. The greater the number of these inconsistencies where the individual has to derive their own conclusions, the greater the potential variance from what was intended by the performance plan.

Even at the individual level of performance improvement planning, it clearly behooves the one developing the plan to ensure that the plan is in alignment with all of the other directional forces at work in the daily environment.

Most performance plans, at whatever level in an organization, more often than not put most of their emphasis on the tactical path and often completely ignore the cultural path or the infrastructure.

When there is a requirement for cultural change, most of the attempts I have seen or read about try to deal with the culture in isolation—as if it is a subsystem that can be separated from the rest. As we discussed in the earlier chapter, this is totally wrongheaded and counter-productive.

And infrastructure, if dealt with at all, is usually limited to some pointed and specific piece that may be totally out of context with the rest of the Alignment requirements—as in the computer service case mentioned earlier in this chapter. It is an interesting side note that in the case of the computer service division, the solution to the organizational performance problem was quick and very measurable. In one year, when the next *Computer Weekly* and *Data Pro Magazine* service rankings came out, the client had moved from last place to first place, and that first place position was maintained for over three years.

In that solution, the two issues that were significantly manipulated were the cultural path and the infrastructure. Very little was done with the tactical path other than to repeat its message as the other two "messages" were significantly altered. And for a service problem that was being measured by *customer* surveys, it is interesting to note that the only employee groups that were *not* a direct focus of the performance plan intervention were the engineers and technicians who actually called on the customers and delivered the measured service. All the changes came about by a focus on infrastructure and culture from the zone manager level and up through the division.

A second aspect of Alignment that also ties into a principle of system is the concept of balance. Each of these directional forces must not only be aligned but must be balanced as well. Each of these directional forces exists for a reason and are in fact critical aspects of organizational functioning.

An attempt to get around the alignment issues by ignoring or devaluing any one of the three directional forces will potentially push the system out of balance, which can result in other aspects of the results formula going haywire. An overbearing drive on the objectives and tasks of the tactical path with little or diminished emphasis on the cultural path can result in an organization that is focused on *getting things done* regardless of the manner, cost in human resources, impact on the environment or customer, or overall propriety.

An overbearing emphasis on the cultural path can result in focus and attention in how people go about work to the exclusion of any focus on the results delivered to the stakeholders. And an overbearing emphasis on policies, procedures, and organizational proprieties can result in employees more focused on internal demands and bureaucracy than on the business plan or results delivered to the stakeholders.

All three directional forces must be firmly grounded in the vision and mission of the organization and further must be in support of each other to deliver the best performance possible, be it at individual, team, group, or enterprise level.

Alignment is about balance and focus within a System (or subsystem) to achieve some stated objective. The Organizational Alignment Professional Committee of the International Society for Performance Improvement has defined Alignment as "coherence of effort across the organization." All that is used, done, and accomplished within the organization must align with the value the organization adds to external clients and society.[5] As a performance improvement professional, making sure there is coherence of effort across all elements of the system is critical and the alignment model is a very useful tool in achieving this coherence.

Endnotes

1. In actual practice, vision and mission are confused and are almost never specific. In addition, popular conventional practice defines a vision in terms of inspirational messages and mission as where the organization is going. Research has shown that although "standard practice," it ignores defining useful results based on performance data (c.f. Davis, 2005, and Kaufman, 2006)

2. This is another example of first defining the ends before selecting the means.

3. Deming, W. E. (1972). Code of Professional Conduct. International. *Statistical Review*, 40 (2), 215-219.

   Deming, W. E. (1986). *Out of the Crisis*. Cambridge: MIT, Center for Advanced Engineering Technology.

   Juran, J. M. (1988). *Juran on Planning for Quality*. New York: The Free Press.

   Kaufman, R. (1991b:Dec.). Toward total quality "plus." *Training*.

4. When there is a disconnect between policies, procedures, and compliance requirements and adding measurable value within and outside the organization, these realities can help you renegotiate them. For instance compliance with a rule that is counterproductive (all paper size must be 8½ x 11 while the standard for your industry and clients is 8 x 10) can be reconsidered).

5. Books one (Kaufman, 2006) and Brethower (2006) relate this to the Organizational Elements where Mega, Macro, and Micro must be aligned and those with Processes and Inputs. Alignment is from external impact to resources.

Chapter 3
Change Management

Change Management has the unique property of being simultaneously one of the least understood and best understood aspects of implementation. The change management "field of knowledge" is fraught with misconceptions, old ideas that have now been shown to be wrong, things that were once true and now no longer apply, and what appears to be simple superstition. Right here at the outset of this topic, let me try to put a stake through the heart of one of the most persistent outright absurdities around this topic. For some reason, there is this belief that people are somehow hardwired to resist change. "People just naturally resist change" is a refrain we all have heard from managers, staff, and even supposed change management experts for years and everyone around seems to smile and nod. What nonsense!

It does not take any fancy research and deep studies to ascertain that this is a fallacious point of view. Just look around in the real world with your eyes only partly open and the irrationality is obvious. People are changing all the time. People are *seeking out* change with high regularity in numerous ways all around you

New products are being brought out regularly and many with outstanding success. When the economy is in an upswing, new cars sell quite well and new housing developments spring up and are quickly sold out. When new and better roads are built, there is not a lack of people wanting to use them. People change jobs with increasing frequency; I have yet to see any patterns of resistance to increased pay and benefits, nor to promotions to jobs where the one being promoted considers it a good opportunity.

Improvements in services are generally warmly embraced, and new businesses, new parks, new computers, new clothes, and new fads continue to occur—and all involve change.

We have moved rather rapidly from records to 8-track tapes to cassettes to CDs to i-Pods; from videotapes to DVDs; from dial phones to push buttons to smaller and smaller cell phones; to voiceover protocols on the Internet. If anything, change is endemic to society in general and is increasing. People do not naturally resist change—particularly when the change is perceived to be for the better!

Quite naturally, people do tend to resist change that appears to make things worse than what currently exists—which should come as no great surprise to anyone.

Changes perceived as a bad move and/or poorly managed change that makes it hard to get things done will indeed provoke resistance—as well it should. In my experience, all too often the refrain from managers that people naturally resist change is nothing more than a way to deny their own culpability in presenting and managing change very poorly.

With the right incentives in place, acceptance of change is easy, not difficult, and not automatically resisted. The operational details of the change may be quite difficult and troublesome, but if the incentive is good enough, that will carry people through and keep them dedicated to successful change Implementation.

If the incentives are not clear or the overall payoff is questionable in the mind of the people impacted, who will want to bother with the effort of changing things—and why should they!

Now with that said, let's move into the topic of Change Management as it relates to Implementation.

Change Management is indeed a fundamental aspect of Implementation. While this topic was also discussed in a previous book in this series (Kaufman, 2006, who also suggests a "partner to the reactive change management" that is proactive "change creation"), I will go over the topic again with particular attention to the critical "dynamic" aspects of Change Management that are central to the Implementation phase.

Change Management is a topic on which much has been written, and there are multiple packages and tools on the market to aid and guide Change Management efforts. From my perspective of looking at Change Management as one of the integral aspects of Performance Improvement—particularly on the organizational level—there are a number of general shortcomings or "positional" problems with the bulk of these offerings.

First, far too many of the producers and authors of these materials approach the topic as a stand-alone activity[1]—as if Change Management were something that could and should be viewed and approached as a topic separate from whatever is being changed; they take a system**s** approach instead of looking at change within and for the entire system—including society—a *system approach*. For many people, the idea seems to be that you analyze your problem or opportunity, design the Performance Improvement approach, and then decide on the Change Management materials you will utilize to aid your Implementation.

The idea of Change Management as a standalone package, concept, or set of tools may be a reasonable, even necessary, approach to addressing the topic as a body of knowledge that can be marketed. However, this approach is not reflective of the reality of applying Change Management knowledge in the most effective manner to facilitate the implementation of a Performance Improvement effort.

Effective Change Management in a Performance Improvement effort should be built into the body of the overall plan. It is not a separate set of tools that are positioned or scattered across various aspects of the Implementation process. Change management should be invisibly and inseparably incorporated into the overall Implementation plan.

While these commercial packages and tools can, at times, still be helpful to a Performance Improvement effort, the reality is that Change Management does not work best as a "bolt on"[1] or addendum to the Performance Improvement effort. To be most effective, the fundamental aspects of Change Management must be designed into the overall effort. In fact, the basic principles of effective change have to be kept in mind from the initial performance intervention data gathering through the analysis and thereby have to be reflected in the final design. In this manner, it becomes integral to the effort, as it should be, rather than an after-market addition.

The logic of this approach is, I would hope, reasonably obvious when a person thinks about it. Unfortunately distilling out the fundamental underlying principles of change management from the abundance of materials on the market is not an easy activity. By the pure fact of putting Change Management into a stand alone package/product, the authors are required to "make a meal" of the topic that while again making sense from a marketing perspective makes it far harder to cut through all the peripheral and supplemental material to ascertain the heart of the matter being discussed. Effective Change Management is not a "Band-Aid" type opportunity—it is both a much larger problem and opportunity.

Further complicating the matter is that Change Management seems to be one of the areas of human phenomenon where the tendency to confuse technology and personal theology seems to run rampant. Long digressions into belief systems about the "nature" of people and "the way they are" based on personal observation and anecdotal recollections are not particularly helpful in sorting out the observable and repeatable underpinnings of Change Management as an activity and arrive at the primary handful of effective change principles.

Based on 30 years of enterprise change efforts in multiple settings coupled with intensive reading of volumes of Change Management materials that have been produced over this same time period, the following provides the four underlying principles that I and some colleagues have distilled out of the massive literature. These four principles have stood us well and are usable from initial data gathering through final implementation. Further, they can be built into the overall Performance Improvement activities.

Four Change Management Principles

Out of all the Change Management theory, research, and experience, there are four fundamental characteristics of effective change efforts that should be incorporated throughout the Implementation process:

1. Increase the benefit.
2. Increase the clarity.
3. Reduce the uncertainty.
4. Reduce the effort.

Before describing the intent of each of these principles, let me address the selection of the two verbs –*increase* and *reduce*—in these four principles. Some of my colleagues take exception to such "fuzzy" verbs and complain that they are not specific enough because they cannot be cleanly measured. How can you tell when it has been done? And that is indeed the point, and why I choose to use these words. There is no point at which you can declare the activity finished or done—no point at which you can "check the box" and declare it done. Rather it is something you do continuously throughout the process at every opportunity. These four activities have more in common with "continuous improvement" than a set business objective.

Now, with the concept of continuous effort toward useful consequences, let's expand on the four principles.

Principle 1: Increase the Benefit. Starting with the basic analysis, you should be looking for benefit and ways to call attention to the benefit. When you are designing the Implementation, you try to point out and underscore the benefits of the change at every opportunity and make the benefits as wide as possible: how the change will benefit the individual, the team, the function, the organization, the customers, the shareholders, the employees in general, and society. This is a search for how many ways the change can provide benefit and look for ways to emphasize each and every one from each and every angle. This focus will align individual payoffs with adding value for all stakeholders.

Keep in mind the point made earlier in this chapter: with the right incentives, change is easy to orchestrate. Clear articulation of the full benefits of the change may be one of the most critical aspects of Change Management and general acceptance and support of the change.

Principle 2: Increase the Clarity. All too often, this aspect is indeed approached as a "set" activity with a beginning and an end. In reality it is, when done properly, a continuous activity. You must be clear, with no appearance of hidden agendas or secret motivations in regard to what you are changing and what you are doing. The reality of this effort is that it is continuous and evolving—particularly in the case of organizational change. The larger the entity of focus for your performance improvement effort, the more dynamic the effort becomes. Achieving clarity is a continuous process. Keep in mind the previous quote that "no plan survives contact with the enemy" and as the performance improvement effort unfolds, things will be changing and you will have to continuously update the clarity efforts. Further, more often than not, the people on the receiving end of your efforts will have clarity requirements you did not anticipate, so another requirement of this principle is the necessity of having feedback mechanisms in place that seek out and advise you of new and/or developing clarity opportunities.

Principle 3: Reduce the Uncertainty. While the above principle is about what you *are* doing, this principle is primarily about what you *are not* doing. This principle is, to a great deal, about rumor control and keeping concerns focused properly. It is, quite frankly, not possible to truly anticipate all the potentially wrong conclusions, interpretations, and extrapolations that people will make from the things you *are* doing. Anything unsaid or not addressed directly can become the fodder for uncertainty. Those same sensors you utilize for uncovering additional requirements for clarity can be calibrated to also provide useful data regarding uncertainties that should be addressed.

Principle 4: Reduce the Effort. The basic principle here is simple. Try and design a change effort that results in it being easier to do things differently than to continue doing them the way they have always been done (while not reducing the results). Often this means as much deconstruction as construction. To return to a point made in the first chapter, patterns of behavior do not occur randomly. If you have predictable patterns of behavior that run counter to the performance you desire, some thing or things are maintaining that pattern. Those maintenance mechanisms required for an existing undesired behavior have to be removed from the System, or at least made more difficult to access and trigger than those put in place to maintain the new desired behaviors.

Now, with the underlying principles in place, there are some additional issues relating to change management that have come to be viewed differently over the past 30 years.

- There are now different approaches for participative change and declarative change.

- There are incremental changes and transformational changes, each with its own patterns and processes.

- Change is now considered endemic to business and society in general rather than the occasional project.

- And through all of this, the requirement for speed in accomplishing desired changes and good results has increased.

Participative Change Methods

The oldest of the documented and validated change methodologies is commonly referred to as Participative Change. There continues to be a fair amount of discussion as to *why* this method works so well, but like many of the ongoing arguments in the psychology/sociology of the human condition many devolve into theological arguments rather than data-based research.

Some say that adults have to be involved in the decision processes to be able to accept changes (Drucker, 1972), some say that the increased involvement increases understanding and therefore makes it easier to accept, others say it is like a pre-emptive close in sales where you co-opt the people into supporting the change, and still others say that the quality of the decisions goes up through involvement and therefore the changes are better planned resulting in higher success rates. And of course, there are those who say the increased success is a combination of some or all of these reasons.

For the purposes of implementation of a Performance Improvement process, we can now, fortunately, avoid the debate and simply look at the relative abundance of data and conclude that for whatever reason, increased levels of active participation in the change process significantly increase the odds of successful Implementation.

This simply means, with one very large caveat, that the implementer should look for and build in as much genuine active participation in the overall change process as possible. The caveat is around active *real* participation. By "real" I mean that the participants can and do actually alter things as a result of their participation. Events orchestrated to give the appearance of participation where in reality the result was a forgone conclusion are not only risky, they can undermine the entire change effort and create focused and energized resistance that otherwise might not have occurred.

While the participative method is highly effective if done correctly, there are some notable downsides to this approach, and they boil down to two primary considerations: time and money.

The time issue is more than just the time involved in orchestrating participation in the process; there is also the issue of sufficient relevant knowledge of the topic under discussion to enable *effective* participation in the process. Getting people sufficiently knowledgeable to take part intelligently in decision making can also add significantly to the overall time problem. In a globalizing economy in the Internet age when competitive time frames are getting tighter and tighter, the amount of time available to achieve a desired change is getting less and less.

Every involvement loop consumes time. If the nature of the involvement is in the realm of decision making regarding the nature and content of a change, the requirement for sufficient knowledge to make considered decisions as well as the requirement for relative expert facilitation also goes up. With the increase in time, there is an increase in cost. Further, an increase in the complexity of what is being decided on will require a concomitant increase in the level of skill required in a facilitator that for most companies will also mean an increase in cost.

Quite naturally, as the speed and quantity of change increases the amount of time available to accomplish required changes is diminishing. The skilled implementer will have to keep these issues in mind when designing the Implementation process.

A different or alternative form of the basic change process has been developed, which is called the *Declarative Change Method*. This methodology was first developed by Operants, Inc., in 1975 as part of a project to implement the Fair Credit Billing Act (passed in 1974) in what were then BankAmericard credit card centers across the country. It was obvious at the time that there was no place for input on whether the law should be implemented or not. Congress had passed the law, and there was a deadline for implementation with serious penalties for failure to do so. *What* was going to change was not open for discussion, nor was the *when* open for discussion. The only discussion point was around *how* the details of the new law were to be put in place by each credit card issuer.

In the years following this successful implementation, the people at Operants and its later off-shoots such as Vanguard Consulting and Vector Group realized that this particular instance was more the norm than the exception when it comes to change in most business organizations. And in the years since, as globalization has increased and global competitiveness has increasingly required faster and faster implementation of required changes, the business requirement for this faster and "limited participation" form of Change Management has steadily increased, even though the commercial Change Management community has been incredibly slow to step up to this demand.

In this approach, the involvement of the target population for the change is consciously limited—usually to participation in deciding/designing the actual implementation rather than involvement in the basic decision making about what will change and when.

What is going to change, when, and why are simply declared with any discussion limited to questions of clarity. Participation in the process is limited to discussions of the best and fastest way to proceed with the declared change. Participation at this level also gets around the "sufficient knowledge" issue as those working where the change is to be put into effect are by definition the most knowledgeable about the immediate impact and what will make the change easier or more difficult to implement.

This approach can dramatically reduce the amount of time required in getting a population up to speed on all the things they must know to be able to knowledgeably take part in discussions about what to change. Further, given the detailed knowledge of the participants around how things get done currently, the facilitation of discussions about how to implement a given change within a given time frame will most often require a far more simplistic level of facilitation, thus saving on both time and required expertise.

The key issue in setting up a Declarative Change effort is in the orchestration of the announcement phase of the change. A convincing reason for the change that is meaningful to the target population is not only necessary, it is critical. And this message must be delivered in a believable manner—which is considerably easier if there is an established high level of trust between the person delivering the announcement (usually a member of the management group) and the population for which the change is targeted. All too often this level of trust has not been developed and the process of increasing trust levels must also be built into the change process.

Fortunately I have found that a well-run declarative change process in the face of real immediate demand can indeed increase levels of trust between management and employee simultaneous with implementing the required changes.

The process of getting ringing clarity on the nature and requirement for change, which is always the first step, is a process that when done properly will often create this new level of candid openness between management and staff that is at the core of a trusting relationship.

Getting clarity requires a process that will enable each and every employee to raise any question, issue, or concern he or she may have and get a considered reply in a timely manner.

A Typical Declarative Change Process

What do you do if you have to effect a large change in operation and do not have the time and/or available expertise and/or money to involve everyone impacted by the change in the decision-making process?

The hard reality of business is that often there are times when organizations cannot consult widely about change but must declare it. Sometimes decisions must be made quickly on the basis of data that are not generally available at all levels of the organization—as when changing market conditions require rapid response to remain competitive. At other times, the decision is not open for discussion—as when legislation mandates non-negotiable changes in policies or work procedure. Under such conditions, it is difficult or impossible to fully involve people in making change decisions in a consultative mode. Unfortunately, there is very little written addressing "declarative" approaches to change, and as a result, many attempts at taking this approach are highly disruptive. Occasionally, the damage done to the organization and its people by the abruptness of the change completely negates its intended positive effect.

I will now describe an approach to implementing a Declarative Change that has been effective in a number of organizations. It of course includes the four basic underlying principles of change discussed above. In addition, it attempts to incorporate, within the declarative model, some of the most effective management and supervisory features and side effects of consultative change.

Research on the factors contributing to effective organizational influence indicates that intervention efforts of whatever type work best when management provides active *support* for the intervention, shares *power* wherever possible, and works to create *trust.*

Support

Key issues in providing support for any intervention are the kind of information provided and the way in which it is provided.

One of the most important elements in providing people with support during a change intervention is full disclosure by management at each phase of the change process. People should have the feeling that their concerns have been heard and that they have the straight story as it affects them. Having given full information, management can further show support by behaving as if they expect full cooperation from the people involved in implementing the change. This acts both to confirm people's belief that they do in fact have full information and that management has confidence in them.

Support is further indicated by the expressed willingness of management to consider adjustments to the Implementation plan and/or other ways of easing the burdens associated with the change.

Finally, support is shown by management's avoiding any subversion of decisions made either at higher or lower levels and acting in a way best indicating their commitment to the change.

Power

Sharing power, when it can be shared, is a key element in influencing change in any organization. One way to do this is to move many of the action decisions as close to the level of final Implementation as possible. There are many opportunities for employees' participation in any major change effort. While the basic decisions may not be open to negotiation or modification, there are almost always a variety of approaches in regard to the *Implementation* of the change(s). Participation, even when limited to this level, not only fosters a feeling of contribution, but improves the efficiency of the Implementation since it is generally employees at the lower levels who have the greatest familiarity with the problems of Implementation that may arise.

Trust

Trust is the most important influence variable. It requires that management not only be open and willing to share information, but also provide an atmosphere of low risk for those who may question the change and/or its impact. A manager who is overly critical can erode this trust. People have to feel they can voice opinions and make suggestions that they will not be penalized for in the future.

Trust also involves the employees' confidence that the management has the ability and the willingness to follow through on commitments and that their contributions are valued and valuable.

Phases of Managing Change

There are three phases involved in implementing a Declarative Change: Preview, Clarify, Implement. Each of these phases may require several steps to accomplish.

PHASE I: Preview (one step)

Preview, as its name implies, is an early view of the proposed change. The general nature of the change, including all non-negotiable decisions is announced. There is no real attempt to answer employees' questions at this time, and little operational detail is provided, since the manager usually lacks the information to do either. What the manager does do at this time is inform the employees of the Clarify process which will follow.[2]

PHASE II: Clarify (three steps: inquiry, analysis, reply)

1. **Inquiry.** In this step, the manager or someone else gathers any questions, issues, or concerns that the employees may have. If the relationship between the staff attending the inquiry session and the manager of the staff is a good one, characterized by high levels of trust and openness, the session can be lead by the manager. If there is not an established high level of trust and openness between manager and the staff, then the session should be facilitated by a neutral nonthreatening party, and the manager of the group should not be present.

   These sessions are done in small groups of no more than 20 people. The reason for limiting the size of the group is to ensure that anyone who has something to say has the opportunity to raise their issues and feels encouraged to do so, while still limiting the time required to solicit and capture any question, issue, or concern. The larger the group, the longer the time it takes to get all questions, issues, and concerns voiced and captured, and the longer the session runs, people begin to tire and tune out.

   The questions, issues, and concerns that are raised must be visibly captured. This can be done by listing them on a flipchart, an electronic board, or some form of projection system. The person gathering the questions captures them in a way that the employee(s) asking the questions or raising the concerns can see it and verify that it is correctly stated. There is no attempt at this time to answer these questions. The point here is to ensure that any and every question, issue, and concern is raised. When answers are provided at the same time, a few things can happen:

- Answers can get quite involved and take up considerable time, and as already stated, the longer the session, the greater the probability that people will tune out.

- With the best of intention, the nature of answers will none the less tend to limit or reduce the nature, manner, and quantity of questions, issues, and concerns that get raised. The purpose of this session is to visibly demonstrate the desire to hear and respond to any and all questions, issues, and concerns so that you want to keep the focus solely on getting them raised and captured.

The inquiry step is concluded when the employees can think of no further questions, issues, or concerns they would like to add to the list.

2. **Analysis.** Questions gathered in each of the groups during the inquiry phase are compiled and reviewed by management and technical experts as appropriate. One result of this step is to create a list of known and, as yet, unknown information required to respond to the questions, issues, and concerns that have been captured. Another obvious aspect of this phase is that the management group can get a good fix on the general "feeling" of the employee group and general nature of their concerns—if any. This overall awareness can help considerably in the planning of the nature and demeanor of how the replies are presented.

3. **Reply.** The reply sessions should occur within 48 hours of the inquiry sessions and will be ideally composed of the same groups of employees. During the reply meeting, it is important for the manager of the group to provide the responses to the questions, issues, and concerns that were raised. This is the opportunity to model being a concerned and responsive leader of the group. It is as important in the reply meeting to say as much as possible of what is known as well as what is not known. The more candid and transparent the information provided and the more candid and transparent the manager appears, the better the session and the more positive the impact on staff/management relations. This includes covering things that you know are not going to happen. This tends to reduce the time that people will spend speculating and thereby reduces the number of incorrect rumors that will inevitably spread. It is very helpful to be able to say or estimate when information that you do not have now is expected to be available. Of course if you do state a future date when an answer will be available, it is critically important to follow through and provide updates as promised.

The Clarify phase most often requires separate meetings to be held for each step. In relatively small changes where the answers are immediately available, it is conceivable that the inquiry, analysis, and reply sessions could immediately follow each other with only a short break in between.

On the other hand, in complex and/or large-system changes, it may be necessary to repeat these three steps as additional information becomes available. This cycle of meetings may be conducted as many times as necessary prior to the implementation phase. One thing that has been noted in implementations of the declarative approach in large systems and/or complex change is that the sophistication of questions significantly increases in repetitions of the Clarify phase. Initially, questions revolve around personal concerns of displacement or disruption, later questions relate to technical issues of the Implementation, e.g., how the System is going to impact the customer service area.

PHASE III: Implementation (three steps: kickoff, monitor, progress check)

1. **Kick-off.** This is a two-part meeting held to inform the group that the change is ready to be implemented and what the final nature of the change is going to be. It is important to achieve and verify ringing clarity on the final nature of the change prior to proceeding to the second part of the meeting. The second part involves the group in making decisions on how to now implement the change in their respective areas.

2. **Monitor.** Monitoring is not a formal meeting, instead it is an ongoing process whereby feedback is solicited/gathered concerning the progress and general success of the Implementation. The monitoring step encourages continued efforts and provides information for any corrective actions or activities that may prove necessary.

3. **Progress Check.** Unlike the monitoring activity above, this *is* a formal meeting to more formally address how things are going. This is a "how are we doing" meeting where each employee reports on the progress made to date. Any problems that have risen over the Implementation period that require a group decision may be raised and modifications made in the Implementation plan. Progress check sessions may be conducted as many times as necessary until the change is fully implemented.

In most instances, as the change becomes fully implemented, these progress check sessions also become the forum for formalizing the shift from formal change Implementation to a focus on Continuous Improvement, which is—or should now be—the norm for most industries and most processes.

As mentioned above, throughout the change process, the four underpinning and guiding principles of any change effort are critical elements that must be continuously applied. In any change, whether it is a Participative Change or a Declarative Change, these four issues represent the core of enabling staff to successfully make the required transition. All management interactions with employees around the change must incorporate the following elements:

- Increase clarity and reduce uncertainty. Encourage open discussion of issues and concerns. Make sure employees know why something has to be done, not just what to do. Touch base regularly with staff to keep them informed and hear their concerns.

- Stress the actual benefits of the change. Create a positive climate by emphasizing what can be accomplished, not what can't. Help staff understand how new programs or policies help support the organization's goals, values, and viability.

- Reduce the effort required by the employees to successfully accomplish the change. Try to simplify complex issues into manageable ones. Avoid the feeling that the "entire world is being turned upside down" by emphasizing what *is not* changing as well as what is changing. Make sure that employees have easy access to support and guidance when and where they can use it to make accomplishing the change as easy as possible.

- Publicize and celebrate progress. Establish milestones and measures by which the employees' efforts may be evaluated. Make it possible for people to see and measure the progress themselves. Review the progress regularly and celebrate the real gains that have been made.

Times of organizational change can be an opportunity to build and enhance the employee/management relationship or severely retard it. Which of the two occurs is dependent not on the nature of the change itself, but on the manner in which the change was carried out. The approaches outlined in this chapter can result in changes being implemented faster than normally thought possible while simultaneously increasing levels of loyalty and trust in the organization. Rapid, successful change that raises levels of commitment to the organization and raises trust in management is the stuff of which competitive edge is made. All of this directly adds measurable value to all in the organization, the organization itself, and the organization's external clients (including society).

Transformational Change

Another Implementation consideration around Change Management is whether the proposed Performance Improvement plan falls into the category of a Transformational Change. A Transformational Change is, by definition, a major transformation in the basic manner of thinking and behaving in the organization.

Business Dictionary.com describes *transformational change* in organizations as follows:

> **transformational change:** In an organizational context, a process of profound and radical change that orients an organization in a new direction and takes it to an entirely different level of effectiveness. Unlike *turnaround* (which implies incremental progress on the same plane), *transformation* implies a basic change of character and little or no resemblance with the past configuration or structure.

Transformational Changes are very substantial shifts in the behavioral makeup of any organization and require relatively intrusive processes to be successful.

A Performance Improvement Implementation that can fall into the category of "continuous improvement" or incremental change is a far easier task and requires far less detail in the planning as it can simply fit into the established processes for continuous learning and change that are already in place in the organization.

Now, in the above paragraph is another subtle truth of Change Management that is critical to the organizational Performance Improvement specialist who has a Performance Improvement plan to get implemented.

The concept of continuous improvement is a value-based proposition that is inherent in what many now call a "learning organization." If the cultural norms in the organization value learning or the continuous improvement of processes and procedures, then an incremental change can be easily put into the existing frameworks for change.

If, however, your organization is like most today and continuous improvement or continuous learning and change is not an embedded aspect of the organizational culture, implementing your Performance Improvement program, however minor the change, may well take on the form of a Transformational Change.

One of the newer understandings of Change Management today is that change is effectively endemic to the business world, and as globalization of the economy increases, the speed of changes will also increase. Change Management can no longer be considered an occasional project—which is how it was originally taught in most business curriculum. Change Management is now a fundamental survival skill for most managers in most organizations. If this concept has not been incorporated on both the skill level and in terms of the corporate culture valuing and embracing change, you most likely have a significant problem that should be dealt with as part of the current change effort.

In today's economy, being a "learning" organization or a company that values and pursues Continuous Improvement is critical to ongoing success. Any organization that does not have this basic aspect to its overall methods of operation is in a decidedly weak position in terms of maintaining market share and competitive position. If the organization is a nonprofit organization, it is in danger of becoming irrelevant in a rapidly changing society, and if a government organization in danger of becoming increasingly inefficient and ineffective in fulfilling its purpose and reason for existence. Anyway you cut it, the organization's future prospects are not good if continuous improvement is not part of its operating norm.

Going further, it would be fair to say that for any organization in any industry today, if it has not yet embraced continuous change into its cultural norms, then this is an aspect that should be built into the performance plan already intended to be implemented. Success of the performance plan will require a transformational effort any way, and adding the value of continuous learning into the change effort will bring additional Performance Improvement—on an ongoing basis—to the organization. In this day and age, an organization's ability to change and adapt with alacrity is an issue central to competitive edge and if not yet in place is simply a necessary strategic change waiting to be requested, so you might as well do it now.

Transformational Changes are shifts in the basic DNA of the organizational culture and require a significant investment of time and energy in that they require the entire management group to systematically rethink and reformulate how they go about accomplishing the business of the organization.

Transformational Change is both a logical process and an emotional process. You are altering the established habit patterns of people across the business, and that is neither a casual nor easy task that can be accomplished in an offhand manner.

The primary aspect of change that comes into play in transformational changes is the necessity of dealing with the emotional aspects of human change. This aspect of change requires a letting go of the past prior to even understanding any required new behaviors, much less implementing them. Dealing with the emotional aspects of Transformational Changes requires a focus on the human emotional change cycle of "endings—transition—beginnings," which is a very different cycle from the traditional and logical business change approach of "present—transition—future" or as is indicated in most business texts "planning—managing—monitoring."

Central to the discussion of the human side of change are two questions that represent most people's initial reaction to almost any significant organizational change:

1. How will this change affect me personally?
2. What's in it for me?

Once clarity is obtained on these two questions, additional aspects of the change can be considered. Until that clarity is achieved, most people find it difficult to focus on other aspects of the change, such as benefits to the organization, benefits to the customers, benefits to society, or even how and when the change will occur.

Successful leadership and management of change require dealing effectively with the human side of change, both in answering these questions for the people being impacted by the change and in dealing with the widely varying individual reactions to the change.

There are four relatively common negative reactions that people may exhibit if the change is not well managed and responsive to the cycle of human emotional reactions to change:

1. **Withdrawal:** indicated by loss of interest, decreased participation, lower energy, and similar indications of simply withdrawing from the overall process

2. **Loss of Identity:** indicated by expressions of confusion, feeling like a number, expressed nostalgia for the good old days, focus on past achievements, and other similar attempts to regain or reassert that they are a person worthy of notice

3. **Disorientation:** indicated by expressions of anger or frustration, confusion, and constant questions about individual assignment and fit in the organization

4. **Disenchantment:** indicated by cynicism, hostile resignation, and expressions of disappointment and anger with the organization

The existence of these types of reactions in people is evidence of the change not being well managed in terms of the human aspects of the change or the emotional aspects of the change. The four principles of change mentioned at the beginning of this chapter are the best defense against these reactions, and increased emphasis and time on those four principles are recommended when these negative reactions become evident.

A manager must recognize the reactions people have to change. The simplest and most direct approach to this potential problem of negative reactions is to ask questions about how the change is affecting them. This should be a regular agenda item on meetings during change efforts, as well as the topic of informal chats with the individuals being impacted by the change.

The manager must continuously work to increase clarity and reduce uncertainty while constantly repeating and under-lining the benefits of the change. In addition, it is imperative that the manager continuously looks for ways to make it easier and easier for the employee to make the necessary changes.

Carefully monitoring the change effort is critical to effective change. As part of the monitoring effort, there are some under-lying responsibilities that fall on the manager throughout the change period:

- Be proactive.
- Anticipate problems.
- Communicate effectively.
- Constantly and consistently ask how the change is going.
- Share information.
- Listen and respond to the "grapevine."
- Be a champion and a good role model for the overall change effort.

Change at the organizational level also has some particular characteristics that make it different from smaller change efforts on a number of levels.

Change in an organizational System may enable other changes to occur, and those changes may be positive or nega-tive. Sometimes the nature of the problem itself shifts to accommodate the changes put in place, and other times new problems may emerge that were simply not visible prior to the change or did not directly exist until the change.

Sometimes other problems could not exist until something else was "fixed" first. A simple example of this is around the general availability of data. When relevant and actionable infor-mation is made available where it previously was not available, issues of what and how to take action can arise for the first time.

The nature of a system as discussed in the first chapter makes all these possibilities a distinct probability. In fact, data developed by W. Warner Burke at Columbia University show that one of the first indications of change progress are both complaints about the change process itself and new problems replacing old problems.

This reality of change in any System also puts to rest another one of the common misconceptions of effective change. Change in Systems will rarely if ever be systematic and orderly. It is an iterative process at best. In fact, it is the iterative nature of change in a System that makes for one of the real challenges calling for good Project Management, which is discussed in the next chapter.

It is not uncommon to discover during the Analysis phase of any particular problem in a System that there are a number of elements involved in getting to a successful conclusion of any given change effort. Often there is a "critical path" of change that has to be followed, where some things have to be changed first that then allow other changes to take place that eventually arrives at the final success of the Performance Improvement intention.

In fact, it is not at all unusual in organizational change efforts that the results of a change will uncover or create "other" problems that did not exist or were not visible previously and will require a new further Analysis, Design, and Implementation.

The concept of "peeling the onion," which is often used in describing the analysis phase of organizational change, actually applies to the entire change process in organizational change—where one aspect of the change uncovers and/or enables another layer of issues and change.

In group or organization change where behavioral alterations are part of the necessary changes, management and leadership as organizational functions come to the forefront. It is impossible to discuss change in the group or organization context without addressing the leadership and management phenomenon. Like it or not, when it comes to organizational performance, it is most often behavioral change that leads to performance change that in turn leads to measurable value added.

In group and organizational settings, successful behavior change and effective leadership go hand in hand. Without even attempting to give full coverage to the issue of leadership—which is a topic all by itself—let me attempt to address, at a very simplistic level, the elements of management and leadership that are critical to effective group and organizational change efforts.

Management and Leadership

If a person is not "doing the work" him- or herself, what do they bring to the work effort? The individual manager/leader provides:

- Direction—clarity on what is supposed to happen and what success looks, feels, and tastes like

- Motivation—a reason or desire for engaging in desired behavior

- Guidance—support and reference for what success looks like and how to get there

When the challenge is to maintain the status quo, the manager is engaging in transactional management:

- Direction is provided by means of goals and objectives

- Motivation is provided by the use of rewards and recognition

- Guidance is provided by coaching, counseling, and training

However, when you are trying to implement a change to the status quo, which is obviously the case when implementing a performance improvement initiative, you are trying to alter established habits. When this is the case, the manager is engaging in transformational management, or what many have come to call "leadership."

When the manager is trying to create a different tomorrow, engage in change, or lead, the actions of direction, motivation, and guidance take on very different behavioral characteristics:

- Direction is provided by a vivid and memorable mental picture of what could or should be. When a manager is trying to get people to a place they have not been before, goals and objectives are not enough. The manager has to paint a picture of what the "new reality" will look, feel, and sound like. This picture of what could be different painted in an appealing manner that leads people to decide that they would like to be a part of that different reality is an important element of direction.

- Motivation is provided by clear standards and positive expectations. This is the oft-talked-about Pygmalion effect that was so vividly characterized in the film *My Fair Lady* when Eliza Doolittle was transformed from a lowly flower girl to a "mannered lady." The manager communicates to those being managed a confidence that the people can indeed accomplish the desired change and that it will be for the better. For whatever reason, people seem to rise to positive expectations—it is a pull rather than a push, particularly when the relationship between employee and supervisor is considered strong and positive.

- Guidance is provided by modeling. In other words the supervisor becomes the model to follow in behaving/ performing in the new desired manner.

Leadership, as described above—providing direction as to where we are going, providing a reason to go and a belief that it is possible to get there, and offering guidance in terms of modeling the desired behaviors—is at the core of successful change in organizations.

Once all the processes and systems are designed and engineered and you are ready to implement the change, it becomes a behavioral issue. Good systems cannot overcome bad people. When all is said and done, organizational change management is about group behavior, and in dealing with group behavior, visible and effective leadership is a critical component.

Project Management/ Change Management Offices

In many companies, offices of this type are a normal appendage to change efforts. On the whole, I have found them to be more problematic than useful in the change effort. Over bureaucratization of "Change Management" and "Program

Management" tends to stultify the entire process, making it less flexible and responsive when success of these efforts requires maximum flexibility and responsiveness, often with a good dose of innovation at regular intervals. Increased levels of oversight and control run counter to what is required.

The basics of Change Management, as they are presented here, should become part of the basic management skill set. Change is endemic and continuous, and the effective management and leadership of change efforts now must be a basic conscious skill set for all managers and supervisors.

When embracing change and leveraging it for the good of the company becomes a basic objective of all management and supervision, you have an organization that is intent on creating and maintaining competitive edge in the market place.

Summary

In summary, responsiveness to change, especially in the rapidly expanding global market, is central to achieving and maintaining competitive edge, and getting the balance of incentives right is central to acceptance of necessary change.

Technology is changing rapidly, and technology drives economics while economics drives society. It is a changing world, and responsiveness to change is central not only to competitive edge, but central to continued existence as a viable organization.

- Change Management is a new "basic knowledge and skill set" for managers in any organization.

- Change Management cannot be left to "specialists," though they can help when in the midst of a major change initiative.

- Change Management is not a "bolt on" piece of a business initiative.

- Change Management must be built into any business Implementation effort and is inseparable from the business process itself.

- Change is not a single "type" of process. There is Participative Change, Declarative Change, Transformational Change, continuous improvement, and various mixes, each requiring its own process for maximum impact in minimal time.

- Change Management requires the management of emotion as well as management of logic.

- Management and leadership are critical components, with specific requirements from people holding such positions, if change is to be successful.

Endnotes

1. A quick Internet search for "change management materials" will suffice to prove the point.

2. This term, I think, was first forwarded by Conner, D. R. (1992, 2006). *Managing at the Speed of Change.* New York: Random House.

Chapter 4
Project Management

The last area of specific knowledge that is often critical to successful Implementation is Project Management. While this is a topic that has *not* been covered in an earlier volume in this series, it is none the less a field of knowledge on which much has been written. Project Management is in fact a specialization all its own. The Project Management Institute offers a considerable amount of training along with an internationally recognized professional certification for professional project managers. If you want more information on Project Management training and certification, it can be found at www.PMI.org. Given this, there will be no attempt to be definitive on that subject within this book.[1] In a like manner to some previous topics, I will only deal with some limited aspects of Project Management solely in regard to Human Performance Technology (HPT) Implementation.

First off, in regard to HPT interventions aimed at individuals, Project Management skills are rarely required, so no time will be spent here dealing with Project Management at the individual performance plan level.

However, as generally unnecessary as Project Management is at the individual performance level, it is usually an *essential* element when the HPT intervention is aimed at group, multi-group, or enterprise-wide and societal value-added performance issues. The larger the group and the more complex the systemic intervention, the more critical good, effective Project Management becomes. But at the same time, when applied to larger HPT interventions, the use of Project Management disciplines is somewhat different from "traditional" Project Management due to the highly iterative nature of group and organizational HPT initiatives. When dealing with systemic performance interventions in large Systems, the process is very rarely (in my experience never) accomplished in a predictable systematic manner.

It is this aspect of HPT projects that is at the center of the "not unusual" amount of friction between the HPT practitioner and the traditional project management professional.

To start with, here is a traditional definition of Project Management from one of a number of Internet sites focusing on Project Management:

Project Management is a carefully planned and organized effort to accomplish a specific (and usually) one-time effort; for example, construct a building or implement a new computer system. Project Management includes developing a project plan, which includes defining project goals and objectives, specifying tasks or how goals will be achieved, what resources are required, and associating budgets and timelines for completion. It also includes implementing the project plan, along with careful controls to stay on the "critical path," that is, to ensure the plan is being managed according to plan. Project Management usually follows major phases (with various titles for these phases), including feasibility study, project planning, Implementation, evaluation, and support/maintenance.

As you can see in the definition, there is a rather strong assumption that Project Management is a relatively linear and straightforward effort of pre-planning and then carrying out that plan in a controlled manner. This is not the "way" of most HPT systemic projects.

In a large-scale systemic performance intervention when you are roughly half way into the intervention, there is a reasonably large probability that at that point you will simultaneously be engaged in some degree of Implementation, some additional Analysis, quite possibly some interim evaluation, as well as additional Design across multiple aspects of the system intervention. The old saying that organizational interventions are like peeling an onion is quite true—each successive layer as you come to it may open up whole new areas, or modify previous assumptions, and/or lead you down entirely new paths in the organization.

This somewhat unique property of group-focused interventions means that it is quite normal that many of the tasks and activities that occur later in the project are virtually unknown during the initial planning phases. In fact, it is not at all uncommon, particularly in large-scale transformations, to build in further analysis and resulting design activities as part and parcel of the later actions in the overall Implementation plan. Quite often some or all of these activities may be performed by select members of the population targeted for the intervention. When activities of this sort are done by members of the target population, it is often in the form of "action learning" or "tiger teams." Groups of managers and/or staff are tasked with researching, analyzing, and resolving issues that surface during the initial Implementation phases of the performance initiative.

Traditional Project Management will most commonly utilize one of the following models. First, and the oldest with its origins prior to World War I, is the Gantt chart:

Gantt Chart: A popular type of bar chart that illustrates a project schedule. Gantt charts illustrate the start and finish dates of the various elements of a project that collectively comprise the work breakdown (or structure) of the project. Some Gantt charts can also show the dependent relationships between activities. For example, if you were implementing a new process for scheduling airline crews for flights, crews could not be selected until after the type of aircraft being used for the flight profile is decided. Crews have to be certified for each type of aircraft they operate, so crew selection is dependent on first deciding what aircraft will be utilized.

Gantt charts can be used to show current schedule status using percent-complete shadings and a vertical "TODAY" line as shown on the following figure. The Gantt chart on the following page shows three kinds of schedule dependencies and percent complete indications.

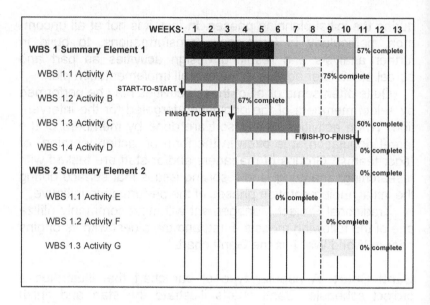

Critical Path Method. Another Project Management approach is the Critical Path Method (CPM), which was initially developed in the 1950s for managing plant maintenance projects.

The Critical Path Method, or critical path analysis, is a mathematically based method for scheduling a set of project activities. It is a method that is today commonly used with all forms of projects, including construction, software development, research projects, product development, and engineering and others in addition to its original use in plant maintenance. Any project with interdependent activities can apply this method of scheduling.

The essential technique for using CPM is to construct a model of the project that includes the following:

1. A breakdown of the work structure

2. The time, or duration, that each activity will take to completion

3. A list of all activities required to complete the project— which is also known as the dependencies between activities

Using these values, CPM calculates the longest path of planned activities to the end of the project and the earliest and latest that each activity can start and finish without making the project longer. This process determines which activities are "critical" (i.e., on the longest path) and which have the greatest degree of flexibility (can be delayed without making the overall project time any longer).

In Project Management, a *critical path* is the sequence of project activities that collectively add up to the longest overall duration. This determines the shortest time possible to complete the project. Any delay of an activity on the critical path directly impacts the planned project completion date (i.e., there is no float on the critical path).

Originally, the Critical Path Method considered only logical dependencies between terminal elements. Since then, it has been expanded to allow for the inclusion of resources related to each activity, through processes called "activity-based resource assignments" and "resource leveling."

Today most uses of CPM are computer based. One of the original computer versions is the Program Evaluation and Review Technique (PERT).

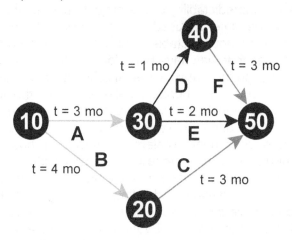

PERT chart for a project with five milestones (10 through 50) and six activities (A through F). The project has two critical paths—activities B and C, or A, D, and F—giving a minimum project time of 7 months with fast tracking. Activity E is subcritical and has a float of 2 months.

Regardless of methodology, be it a simple spread sheet, a Gantt chart, CPM, PERT, or Microsoft project (a very common hybrid of the above methods), traditional Project Management is founded on the principle of thorough planning of the project *from start to finish.* This plan is then carefully tracked and routine reports are generated, documenting progress as well as reporting on identified or anticipated problems.

In short, a typical Project Management System lists all the tasks, usually in order of initiation or in categories of work or responsibilities. Each task has an initiation and target end date and parties responsible and/or involved are identified. Interdependencies are usually noted, from which a critical path could be determined if desired.

For the average project manager, or at least all those whom I have worked with, this projection and percentage-done reporting and accountability process is one of the more powerful and central elements of effective Project Management. And, of course, therein lies the rub.

When Project Management comes face to face with HPT as applied to groups, and particularly when applied to enterprise interventions, the two processes do not appear to match up. The inherent unpredictability of the project activities themselves, much less the time required to accomplish those activities coupled with the unpredictable nature of even the content and scope of things that may have to be "dealt with" toward the latter stages of the project, makes the "traditional" focus of Project Management somewhat nonsensical—at least on the surface.

As has already been noted, group and enterprise HPT interventions are almost always iterative; they are self-correctable. Where a "proper" project, in terms of basic Project Management, is well planned and systematic in nature, performance trouble shooting and intervention at the enterprise level is never systematic. Adjusting one aspect of a system quite often uncovers other aspects that were previously hidden, or clouded, prior to the "fix." Evaluations of interventions often lead to new areas of concern. When dealing with complex and cross-functional activities, even the announcement of *intended* changes may trigger the uncovering/identification of additional areas of inquiry and potential change.

As was stated above, it is not particularly unusual for an enterprise performance intervention to unfold such that the HPT practitioner may be evaluating one part, implementing another part, designing yet a third, and just beginning an analysis into a fourth, and the only part that was in the initial project design was the first element.

So given all this, you may well ask why I stated in the beginning of this chapter that effective Project Management is usually an *essential* element when the HPT intervention is aimed at group, multi-group, or enterprise-wide issues. The answer is that the value comes in other aspects of proper Project Management rigor and is something a good seasoned project manager can readily appreciate *once they understand* the very different iterative nature of typical large System HPT projects and how each layer and level of the organization (onion) must link, align, and add value within and external to the organization.

The iterative nature of both group and enterprise-wide HPT interventions cries out for a robust methodology to capture and track all the various threads that continue to present themselves as the HPT practitioner engages in dealing with and resolving more complex systemic performance problems.

Where most traditional Project Management focuses on the predictive and controlling nature of a project as it moves systematically through to completion, in group and enterprise HPT projects, the focus is more on where you have been and how and why you got there along with assuring that the various threads that are uncovered are not lost and the inter-connections are documented and tracked.

A traditional Project Management meeting will focus on degrees of completion and variance from the plan with actions planned to get back onto the plan. In an HPT intervention at the group or enterprise level, the focus will be on capturing the unexpected and figuring in the consequences of these new unanticipated elements both within and outside of the organization.

While these two aspects are similar if you step back and look at it, the nuances of difference are significant enough to make the average project manager uncomfortable. The nature of what it means to "keep the project moving" is subtly different from the traditional project focus of "staying" or "getting back" on track that is the normal focus of Project Management. The mind set of the traditional project manager is more on control and accountability, particularly in relation to keeping the project on topic and on time. In the HPT project, the focus is primarily on documenting the changes and additions and connections. The project team is routinely revising what the activity tracks are and refiguring the overall project scope and time lines.

Another way of putting this is that when applying Project Management to an enterprise HPT project, it is task dynamic rather than task static. The only relatively stable anchor point is the desired result, not the elements in getting to that desired result. Like everything else in HPT, and as is mentioned repeatedly throughout this series of books, the focus is on the results and consequences, not a blind adherence to some foreordained process—results and consequences, not compliance.

It is important to point out that even given what has been pointed out above this does not mean that the control and predictability aspects of Project Management are ignored. That is far from the case. Like any other project, the initial activity in Project Management is specifying the scope, identifying all the known elements or activities of the project, identifying necessary resources (staff, time, budget, tools), and plotting those resources against the project plan. In fact, it would be fair to say that this is part of the problem with the average project manager who is unused to an HPT project. The HPT project seems to start out the same as any other project, so they can easily settle into the assumption that this project is no different from any other project.

The differences manifest themselves as the project unfolds. Any project, including non-HPT projects, may well have new activities uncovered in the course of the project, resulting in the project having to be modified. And, even in HPT projects, at each project review, you will be trying to anticipate (predict) what else will have to occur and what the processes and time lines will be and revise the project plan to reflect these changes. The difference comes in the relative time and focus. In the traditional non-HPT project, the primary focus is on control and attempting to keep on the predetermined path and time line. In the HPT project, the primary focus is on what has happened and understanding the consequences. Critical paths can shift dramatically and require re-allotment of resources and focus, and each new area of interest will add additional nuances and connections that must be captured and documented. Both activities, looking back and documenting (as well as planning ahead), will occur, but the relative emphasis is reversed. In addition, in an HPT project, there will be some activities where the detail of the process, the specific content, and the time required to complete it will be intentionally vague with only broad outlines, which is anathema to the traditional project manager. What will help the new project manager in adapting is to realize both

- the variability involved in dealing with people and their emotions, memories, expectations, anticipations, and prejudices, and

- the absolute criticality of understanding where the project has been and why, which provides crucial information in regard to managing and maintaining the operation after the Implementation is completed and how each building block result adds total value.

Whenever the enterprise performance intervention is done, there will be a new dynamic balance established, and maintenance of that balance will require a knowledgeable management that is aware of the interrelations between the pieces of the reworked System. The documentation that is provided by a good Project Management System can be critical in ensuring that this knowledge is not lost and newly discovered or understood threads and connections are not forgotten or overlooked in the eventual completion of the HPT project. This knowledge can be vital in guiding the understanding and ongoing maintenance of the overall system.

When implementing a new software system, or installing a new piece of machinery, or implementing a new process flow, the focus is usually on how the target System or sub-system and its new element(s) are designed and how it all fits into the rest of the existing elements in a mechanical way.

By definition, no HPT project will be mechanical at its core. If people are involved, the people will be the critical element, and people are not mechanical nor necessarily logical or even practical. HPT deals with sub-systems that are part of a *living* System. Many critical "cogs" in a living System are sentient, not inanimate objects. The focus in an HPT group or enterprise System must be on understanding the nuances of how the pieces, particularly the human pieces, *behave* rather than simply the task(s) they perform. All the parts of any living System, human and organizational, work independently and also interact. The interactions are essential to successful project Implementation and success.

Additionally, when compared to mechanical Systems, living Systems are far more dynamic and will potentially have considerable variance built in as part of the overall system potential. People in the System are dynamic, not static, and understanding and tracking the ongoing behavior and interdependencies, and allowing for them, are far more critical than any set algorithmic intent or design.

This whole dynamic nature of HPT projects is particularly obvious in the Change Management phase of the project. I have always found it curious that in HPT we always seem to acknowledge the requirement for a Change Management phase without really giving any thought to the nature of Change Management in human beings.[1]

When all is said and done, the core of Change Management when dealing with System changes that involve people is around uncovering and managing the emotions that are inevitably involved when humans are asked to move from the familiar and known into the relatively unknown.

There is a great quote from *The Prince* by Machiavelli that I have used often as part of a Change Management exercise that does a nice job of summing up the nature of change when people are involved.

And it ought to be remembered that there is nothing more difficult to take in hand, more perilous to conduct, or more uncertain in its success, than to take the lead in the introduction of a new order of things because the innovator has for enemies all those who have done well under the old conditions, and lukewarm defenders in those who may do well under the new.

While the logic of a change effort will, on the surface, lend itself to Project Management, the emotions that emerge in the change process will not. The only view from which the change process applied to humans is a systematic process is in one of those "50,000-foot" views that strategists and planners often talk about. From enough distance, the process or pattern is somewhat clear, but as you get into the detailed topography of actually getting from one place to another, the seemingly unpredictable variability becomes more obvious than does the overarching high-level pattern of the general process.

In other words, while the general pattern of the Human Change Cycle does lend itself to Project Management in a traditional sense, the emotions that will emerge and the detailed aspects of dealing with them are highly variable in both detailed content and in terms of time required and as such *do not* lend themselves to traditional Project Management.

Change Management, and for that matter management and supervision in general, is a heuristic process, not an algorithmic process. This is a concept that has escaped most people in our field.

Webster's Unabridged Dictionary provides the following definition for *heuristic:*

Main Entry: [1]**heu·ris·tic** Pronunciation Guide

Pronunciation: '(h)yù|ristik, -yü|-, -tēk

Function: *adjective*

Etymology: German heuristisch, from New Latin heuristicus, from Greek heuriskein to discover; akin to Old Irish fūar I have found: providing aid or direction in the solution of a problem but otherwise unjustified or incapable of justification <heuristic techniques> <a heuristic assumption> <even vague and dubious assertions can render good services to empirical research as a

heuristic stimulus—Edgar Zilsel>; specifically : of or relating to exploratory problem-solving techniques that utilize self-educating techniques (as the evaluation of feedback) to improve performance <a heuristic computer program>—**heu·ris·ti·cal·ly** \-tək(ə)lē, -tēk-, -li\ adverb

– "heuristic." *Webster's Third New International Dictionary, Unabridged* (2002). Merriam-Webster, http://unabridged.merriam-webster.com.

In management and supervision, as well as in Change Management and in HPT large System interventions, there are always multiple paths to the same end. The precise path taken in any given situation is variable and to a great degree dependent on the often unpredictable reactions of the various parties involved as the process unfolds. When there are multiple potential paths to success and the proper path depends on the circumstances of the moment, you cannot take a set cookbook (an algorithmic) approach. You have to have guidelines that suggest how to proceed, taking into account the unique variables of that situation at that time. The development of these guidelines, a heuristic, is quite a bit different from a set solution.

When you look at the standard Project Management models, such as the Gantt and PERT chart examples above, multiple paths to the same end are not an easy fit.

It is fair to say that traditional Project Management, particularly as practiced by the novice or relatively inexperienced, does not easily translate to heuristic processes. Project Management tends to be taught and practiced in an algorithmic manner, and those used to algorithmic process will require some time and considerable thought to adapt the still necessary aspects of good Project Management when applied to the heuristics of dealing with emotional situations and management and supervisory issues.[3]

Yet another nuance of Project Management in HPT applications occurs in many large-scale performance interventions when the process leans on "bottom-up" logic rather than external pre-analysis. Bottom-up logic is an approach that focuses and depends on accessing the knowledge and experience of the people involved in the actual performance of targeted and related tasks.

This approach takes on many of the characteristics of "emergence" as referenced in complexity theory.[4] The science of complexity is about looking for the general law of pattern formation in a non-equilibrium System. Organizations are by definition complex Systems. There are a great many independent agents interacting with each other in multiple ways. It is the very richness of these interactions that allows the System as a whole to undergo *spontaneous self-organization*. This is particularly true of living Systems. Living organisms are constantly adapting to each other. In every case, groups of agents seeking mutual accommodation and self-consistency somehow had to transcend themselves, acquiring collective properties that they might never have possessed individually. Furthermore, these complex, self-organizing systems are adaptive, in that they don't just passively respond to events the way a tree limb sways in the breeze. They actively try to turn whatever happens to their advantage. The human brain is constantly organizing and reorganizing its billions of neural connections so as to learn from experience (in broad terms). Humans adapt to better survive in a changing environment—and so do corporations and industries. The corporation's external and internal environments are constantly changing. The marketplace alone is responding to changing demographics, technological developments, shifts in supply and demand, and a host of other factors.

Living Systems are complex organizations, and complex organizations are adaptive, either overtly or covertly, and as such always changing. They have a dynamism that makes them qualitatively different static Systems that are merely complicated. Complex Systems are more spontaneous, more disorderly, more **alive**. Yet, at the same time, they are not chaotic. Complex Systems have the ability to bring order and chaos into a kind of balance—a self-organizing cohesiveness.

It is from this reality that the concept of "the answers are in the System" has its base. If you want to know how things *really* work in the organization or how they *could* really work, you go to the parts of the System that are involved in the area of investigation. This is the bottom-up approach. Exactly what it will look like and what is involved are not really known until you get into the situation.

The nature of Project Management changes when the activities, tasks, and related behaviors emerge from the bottom up rather than from the top down. The details evolve out of the interactions of the people as they address or rethink processes, or means, to get a given result.

In these approaches, precisely what will come up is unknown when the process is begun and the initial task of the good project manager is to capture "live" the various threads and ideas as they emerge from the interactions of the group when they initially engage in any given task.

Large group re-engineering (reorganizing the operations for greater efficiency) is a classic example of this approach.[5] Precisely what elements of any given process flow will be re-engineered is unknown at the beginning of the activity. A good dynamic project manager will understand that a big part of the Project Management role is capturing all the elements of the overall process as they come up and turning each into a mini project with interdependencies identified as they emerge from the group interactions.

Additionally, as has been mentioned previously in the chapter on System, the beginning stage of projects in a System, particularly in a living System, is induction rather than deduction. The first stage of a project of this nature is a steady expansion of what is to be dealt with and included in the overall project, and the documentation and tracking of this is critical to eventual success.

The parts of traditional Project Management that come closest to reflecting what Project Management looks like in an HPT project is the "beginning project activity" as mentioned earlier and in the "end of project" activity where the history of the project is reviewed and "lessons learned" are captured for future reference.

The end of project activity is the more accurate reflection of the value of Project Management rigor in enterprise-wide projects than is "schedule tracking" of traditional projects. It is often helpful to point out this similarity to your project manager in the beginning of the relationship to help them recalibrate their expectations of how they will add value to the project.

When dealing with heuristic processes and/or iterative processes, the project rigor of a clearly stated final result is, if anything, even more important than it is with algorithmic projects. The trick is to have a firm focus on the final result and ensure that the desired outcome is reached and that all the interrelationships are documented, rather than ensuring that some predetermined series of steps are slavishly followed. But in building a good heuristic process, it is critical to capture and document the various indicators that help guide the process in ensuring that the desired outcome is achieved.

Capturing and documenting these indicators are critical pieces of enabling ongoing management of a dynamic living System. In many ways, a living System never really settles down into a narrow and predictable mode of operation—or at least not to the degree that is obvious in a mechanical System. There is predictability, but the variance in how the System operates is far greater, and the predictability of the process can only be ascertained by taking a more "distant" view.

Once again, we are back to the "50,000-foot view" rather than a detailed up-close view. It is only through repeated events that a general pattern will emerge since each individual event will exhibit differences. Getting too close and detailed around any single event will obscure the patterns rather than guide the observer to recognize the patterns.

Within the Human Change Cycle, there are processes that are designed to surface emotions and allow them to be managed. While the beginning and end of the process are clear, precisely what will come up, how long it will take, and what subroutines will be involved in working through it are *not* known in advance. This is why these processes are indeed heuristic in nature, having numerous potential paths to the desired outcome.

It is difficult at best to project manage a process. But particularly when "time required" is a variable based on content that is unknown at the beginning of the process, much of the rigor and subsequent predictability of traditional Project Management become impossible.

Project Management in HPT is effectively a trailing event or a recording/documenting activity. You want to know where you went, what was uncovered, and why so that no threads get lost and the management charged with maintaining the changed processes once Implementation is complete are aware of the elements to which they have to pay attention as they proactively manage the System. The traditional predictability properties of Project Management that are dependent on operational detail are simply not available.

Most organizations do not have a good documentation of their organizational system and its interdependencies, which quite frankly is often at the core of well-intended but misguided management of organizations. The complex interdependencies of larger organizations are not necessarily obvious and are easily overlooked when not clearly documented. This results in decisions getting made or actions taken without a real awareness of all that is going to be impacted. This can also result in increasing organizational inefficiencies.

In large and complex Systems, people tend to focus only on the part that they see, with little thought given to anything outside of their area of responsibility. This can occasionally result in serious waste and inefficiency.

A classic example of this occurred a few years back when doing a Performance Improvement project in a large credit card center.

Merchant drafts came into the center every day and, over a 24-hour period, were processed and credits deposited into the various merchants' bank accounts.

A number of changes had occurred in how merchant drafts were processed over the years since the initiation of credit cards and there had never been a systemic review of the entire merchant draft processing system. If you are unfamiliar with the term, *merchant drafts* are the items that the merchant sends to the bank to get credit for purchases made with credit cards. The piece of paper you sign at the

(continued)

retail outlet is the "draft" that the merchant deposits with his or her bank to get reimbursed for the purchase you made.

Like many aspects of credit card processing, this particular aspect had not been addressed in many years. The nature of credit cards at that time was that through the year, you got a steadily increasing volume month by month that peaked in December. The volume would then drop off in January, but by March, the total volume would be equal to what it was the previous December. The net result was over 20 years of increasing volume with little time to step back and review how things were being done. All the effort of management was focused on constant growth and adaptation to simply keep up.

When analyzing and documenting the merchant draft process, one of the flows involving merchant drafts from gas stations had a step in the process where a number of copies of the draft were made at different points in the process and centrally filed.

No one that we interviewed in the credit card merchant processing section knew precisely why the copies were made, nor who, or under what circumstances, the copies were accessed. As the operation was a 24-hour process with different aspects of the processing occurring on each shift, everyone assumed that whatever was done with the copies occurred on a different shift.

Nothing in the analysis indicated there was any particular problem or sensitivity with the copies, so it was not immediately dealt with in the redesign, and that piece of the process was left unchanged. At the end of the project, as part of a final check, every change had to be signed off on by each group that was directly or indirectly involved in the merchant draft process.

Since the merchant processing included making and filing these copies, clearly someone was using them at some point, so in the end we had to check to make sure

(continued)

that none of the changes in process that we were intending to implement had a detrimental or unintended impact on them. If not for the Project Management rigor of capturing all the related "threads," we might have never come back to this particular point in the process.

To get this final signoff—something we considered to be a formality rather than any central efficiency issue—we had to find out who used these copies. This investigation took somewhat longer than anticipated. In fact, after considerable effort and much to our surprise, we discovered that one of the greatest potential impacts on efficiency in processing merchant drafts was in this copying and filing part of the system.

As it turned out, there was indeed a rational reason for the copying and filing, but it was literally 20 years old. We now had a room that measured roughly 25 feet by 100 feet that was filled with files that nobody accessed. As far as we could determine, these files had not been accessed in over 10 years. Back when they *were* used, it occurred on the swing shift when there were almost no managers, and certainly no senior managers, working, so no one of note had noticed this interesting fact.

In a project focusing on efficiency, the greatest single impact came as a result of the Project Management documentation and following up on a thread that we did not think was all that vital.

One of the great values of proper Project Management documentation is that it can capture the interdependencies and document the interrelationships that are required for the organizational intent to be realized. The more the management group can understand the complex interrelationships and interdependencies involved in carrying out the organization's intent, the more effective the management will be in guiding, monitoring, and supporting these organizational activities.

For the HPT practitioner, it is quite important when preparing for a group or enterprise intervention to have an in-depth meeting with your project manager well in advance of initiating the project, particularly if the project manager has not previously worked with these types of projects. You will have to go over the aspects of Project Management discussed above and assure the project manager that he or she is indeed important and critical to success, but the nature of his or her involvement and where he or she will add significant value is different from what he or she may be used to doing.

I can say from personal experience that developing a positive relationship with a good project manager who can learn and appreciate the differences can become a highly useful partnership that will add immense value. But taking on a project manager who is inexperienced with this approach at the beginning stages of a project will often lead to upset and even overt acrimony at a time when your full focus must be on your customer and running the project. Once you begin the actual project is the time at which you can least afford distractions within your own team, so deal with these issues well before you get into the task of actually running a project.

Summary

Project Management and Change Management are about guiding a dynamic set of people and an organization in the direction of what was defined as useful results both inside and outside the organization. It is holistic and not fragmented, and there are concepts and tools to help you and your organization get from "what is" to "what should be" and be able to prove internal and external value added.

Endnote

1. A quick check at www.pmi.org, or a Google search under "project management" will provide abundant resources for those who wish to look into this area in more depth.

2. The first book in this series (Kaufman, 2006) also discusses a "twin" of Change Management termed change creation. Change Management is reactive, and change creation is proactive. Both are vital.

3. The heuristic concept is also discussed in a more expanded manner in chapter 5 of this book.

4. Emergence is the arising of novel and coherent structures, patterns and properties during the process of self-organization in complex systems. A good short article on Emergence can be found in the internet Wikipedia.

5. Re-engineering—the fundamental rethinking and radical redesign of business processes to achieve dramatic improvements in critical contemporary measures of performance, such as cost, quality, and speed.

Chapter 5
Assuring Clarity and Ability

The first active step in implementing an HPT improvement plan is to ensure that the person or population being targeted by the plan, **and any others who have a direct or indirect impact on that target and/or the ability to implement the plan**, are fully aware of what is intended and how it applies to them. It should come as no shock that awareness must precede implementing the plan.

Until this clarity is achieved, it is often impossible to ascertain whether or not the target (be it an individual, a team, a department, or an organization) has the ability to perform as desired—to add value within the organization as well as to our shared society.

Usually the direct target of the intervention does get some amount of clarity prior to being expected to implement, but over the years, I have to admit to more than one instance in which the analysis showed that no one told the target group clearly what was expected.

The more common gap relates to the persons referred to in bold in the first paragraph above—others (not the immediate target) who have direct or indirect impact on the target. This is particularly true in relation to groups upstream and downstream of the targeted activity and the secondary impact of the change on them.

Clarity has a number of components:

1. Are the employees aware that the performance is expected?[1] While I will grant that it is not so common that it can be called routine, it is still surprising to me how often an analysis will show that the desired performance was never clearly asked of the employees.

2. Has the desired performance been specified sufficiently that the performers know what to do and how it will be measured? Do they agree that the results will be valuable for all stakeholders? A far more common problem is that the desired performance has not been stated in clear terms that help guide the performance. Often the

metrics are also unclear or unavailable to the performers, which can add to the feeling of uncertainty about what is *really* expected.

3. Are those who formally or informally routinely interface with the performers aware of and support what the performers are expected to do? Are the managers and supervisors aware of and managing/supervising in a manner to reinforce and support the desired performance? What about other people or groups working around the target group who can directly or indirectly influence the performance of the target group? Humans are social animals and highly susceptible to the views and feelings of those they work with and around.

4. Are all individuals and/or groups with any interdependency on the targeted performance aware of and support the expectations? What about the people who provide the inputs for the target group or receive the outputs of the target group—are they aware of and supportive of the desired performance?

All too often efforts to make the desired performance clear are too limited in their scope and are aimed only at the immediate performer with no thought to the social and political environments within which the jobs are performed.

Ability, like *clarity* above, has a number of components, and all must be checked for alignment with the desired performance.

By *ability* I mean both are the staff *able* and are the staff *allowed* to perform as desired or do the following conditions exist?

- Skill deficiencies

- Perceived deficiencies (lack of confidence or assumed lack of skill/ability)

- Resource constraints

- Environmental restraints
  - physical
  - social/interpersonal

- Management/supervision practices not aligned with the performance and internal as well as external value added

- Conflicting behaviors that have higher value

How this assuring of clarity and ability is best done varies based on the nature of the work and whether the target is an individual, a team, a group of teams, or an entire organization. Clarity comes from many sources, and it begins with clarity on the analysis. In the traditional Human Performance Technology (HPT) interventions that focus on an individual job, a thorough understanding of the job is derived from both the initial analysis and is usually further understood and clarified as a side effect of the design and test process. In the initial days of HPT—well before we ever called it HPT—when the focus was on validated methods for instilling necessary skills and knowledge in the people performing any given task, we often talked about understanding the job "down to the operant level." This is a rigor that rarely exists now, and in fact, the whole underpinning of what "down to the operant level" means has been lost. Our roots in rigorous behavioral analysis are rarely taught, even at the Master's level in today's instructional design programs—and the "cost" in terms of accuracy, thoroughness, and sustainable impact are quite notable.

Equally, an alternative path that leads to the same degree of thoroughness that came out of industrial engineering—methods analysis including time and motion studies—has also fallen into obscurity. There are a number of factors that play into this sad state of affairs, some rational and some not.

In the not-rational category, one of the greatest examples is embedded in the rise of the term "Taylorism" as a negative epithet. *Taylorism,* or in many American circles also referred to as *Fordism* for Henry Ford's application of Taylor's principles, refers to the body of work of Frederick Taylor which was initially captured and presented in his work *The Principles of Scientific Management* published in 1911.

Taylorism as a negative derives from a rather significant misinterpretation of Taylor's work as dehumanizing. If you take the time to read his work, *and* read it within the context of the times in which it was written, the absurdity of this dehumanizing label is quite obvious. In fact, the truth is quite the opposite. In far too many companies, management grossly misapplied and distorted the principles, and the burgeoning union movement, which was to a great extent a direct result of this wrong-headed use of his work, focused on these distortions and painted the entire body of work with the same negative brush. Let's take a moment and review the central points of Taylor's work. Listed below are Taylor's four principles of Scientific Management:

1. Replace rule-of-thumb work methods with methods based on a scientific study of the tasks

2. Scientifically select, train, and develop each worker rather than passively leaving him or her to train him- or herself

3. Cooperate with the workers to ensure that the scientifically developed methods are being followed

4. Divide work nearly equally between managers and workers so that the managers apply Scientific Management principles to planning the work and the workers actually perform the task

I contend that anyone would be hard pressed to find anything "dehumanizing" in these four principles. Rather than being dehumanizing, these are principles that if followed properly will increase the humanity of the work environment.

Much of the rigor and processes involved in planning and implementing a successful work System was first captured in Taylor's Scientific Management approach. The emotional attacks on Taylor generally stem from the incorrect and distorted use of some of the tools Taylor used in his Scientific Management. The tools were utilized by some employers to distort the balance that Taylor had in mind and instead were utilized to increase usurious and one-sided approaches to work design where all the pluses went to the owners and less and less went to the workers.

This has resulted in the tools and methods being viewed as negative approaches to enable exploitation of the workers rather than enlightened balance. What we require today is a return to many of the methods and tools of Scientific Management but applied clearly within the concepts of balance and fairness. Time and motion studies as well as methods research (now often labeled re-engineering) are overdue in returning to the HPT kit bag.

A common term in HPT today is *subject matter expert,* or SME. Years ago, when I first heard the term it was rather simple in concept. SMEs were people currently performing the job well (also referred to as exemplars) and/or those currently performing the job at the current average levels of performance.

In my early days, coming out of industrial/organizational psychology, the SMEs, and preferably exemplars if available, were the people you watched and questioned as you bore down to the operant levels of behavior and/or you observed during your time and motion study and then questioned as you completed your methods analysis.

For those coming out of the early instructional design days, the SME was the person who had the most knowledge regarding the "content" of the course being designed. If the course was on map reading, an SME would be a person most knowledgeable about all the things that could and should be ascertained from reading a map.

Somehow the term *SME* has broadened over the years and now, quite often, will embody "previous" performers who are currently viewed as being outstanding performers back when they did that job, or people who are "responsible" for the job or jobs in question, which is somehow viewed as equating to being an expert on the content and performance of the job.

As Roger Kaufman observed to me recently, applying the term to people of this sort requires changing the SME definition to "Subjective Matter Experts," and he has the research to substantiate his redefinition.

The point being, if you intend to have viable HPT interventions, your analysis must center on robust data from *current performers.* Not expert observers, not past expert performers, not people "very knowledgeable" for whatever reason, but people currently *performing* the task or tasks that are the focus of the analysis.

It is also useful, and almost always necessary, to routinely gather data from management, peers, and representatives of all those interacting directly or indirectly with the performers. This expansion beyond the individual performer is most critical when dealing with group, function, or larger performance issues. Clarity is contingent on an accurate and robust understanding of the actual performance of the task(s) as well as an accurate and robust understanding of the context within which the tasks are being performed. As a reminder, what is meant by "context" is covered quite thoroughly in the first chapter on System.

When analyzing a job or function, it is important to make sure the "total" job or function is represented. All too often in recent years with the combination of time pressures, competitive urgency, and limited resources, it is no longer possible to engage in the time-consuming approaches of methods research or operant level specification. Adding to this is the increasing frequency and requirement for HPT solutions focused on entire process or "value chains" that involve multiple jobs, tasks, and performers. I have been tasked with improving processes where attempting to do the types of task by task data gathering I did in my early years would have added weeks, if not months, to the basic data-gathering efforts. In this modern day of global competition and rapid technological change, that amount of time is, in most instances, simply not available if you wish to be competitively viable and responsible.

When the HPT practitioner is charged with reducing cost and time in supply chain management, or improving the productivity and quality of a value chain (the route taken through the organization as "raw materials" are transformed into a delivered good or service), there is almost always a very limited time available to do the data gathering. It is not unusual that "as good as it gets" is the ability to interview, for an hour or two, one exemplar, or a couple of average performers, for each link in the overall process or value chain.

This reality makes it imperative to maximize both the quality and quantity of information you derive from each opportunity to gather information about the performance(s) under investigation.

Here are two relatively simple tools and one somewhat complex approach or process that I have found very helpful in achieving maximum quality and quantity in limited time when in the analysis/understanding phase of HPT design. And remember, the point here is that a thorough understanding of the targeted performance is a fundamental enabler to ensuring sufficient clarity.

The two tools are both interview aids. First off, when interviewing job incumbents as stated previously, often you have no more than an hour or two to complete your interview. If you simply ask them to describe the job, you will rarely get a complete picture. They will often focus on the more overt or obvious aspects of the job and with no malice of forethought, overlook many aspects of the job that may well be the critical pieces you have to acquire and then provide complete clarity.

The use of a simple job model will help stimulate recall when doing a job or function analysis.

One such job model is the predictability/time delay grid. All jobs and functions have four aspects to job performance. There are tasks or parts of the job that can be predicted in advance and those that cannot. There are tasks that when called on to perform them the employee has to respond immediately and others that can be delayed and performed at some later point in time. Putting this into a simple model gives you a grid like that below.

PREDICTABILITY/TIME DELAY GRID

	Immediate Performance	Delayed Performance
Predictable	Routine	Administrative
Unpredictable	Emergency	Project

Using this grid as a reference tool for the job incumbent during the interview will significantly enhance the thoroughness of the information provided in your limited time frame.

Let me add a quick note about the above grid. Please focus on the axis and what each box *represents* in terms of task characteristics, not the labels in the four boxes. If those labels don't work for you, change them.

By laying out the above grid to Subject Matter Experts, or job incumbents, and asking the interviewee to address all four areas, a more thorough and complete description than you would otherwise have gotten is the usual result.

The first step is to ask the performer to put an estimated percentage of time spent in each of the quadrants in the average day, week, or month. Then the second step is to fill in the detail of the tasks that reside in each of the categories.

The second tool is a model to help in formulating questions and organizing data. When dealing with any system, particularly complex systems like organizations, it is critical to have some form of guiding methodology for assuring that you are not overlooking any relevant aspects of the system and for organizing your data.

In performance improvement situations, we are dealing with the dual aspects of the actual work combined with the social-cultural aspects of people doing work. To respond to this, we developed a model based upon these two perspectives. One perspective is the industrial engineering model of work, which is described as a set of conditions, within which a process occurs that results in an output:

Conditions ⟶ Process ⟶ Results (Products, Outputs, Outcomes)

The other perspective is the sociological view of work, which is that work is performed by people within an organization. The combination of both approaches gives us a nine-box model that reasonably represents the organizational system:

	Conditions	Process	Consequences
Organization	**Direction** • Business situation • Vision/mission • Strategy, tactic • Structure • Goals and objectives	**Procedures** • Planning • Policy/procedure • Support • Information subsystems • Budgeting • Monitoring	**Results** • Success measures • Societal value added • Profitability • Competitive position • Stakeholder Satisfaction
People	**Values/Beliefs** • Ideal values • Actual values • Climate • Objectives/demands • Expectations • Politics	**Leadership/Management** • Practices/behaviors • Selection/development • Reward/recognition • Skill/knowledge • Motivation/feedback	**Productivity** • Performance levels • Morale • Empowerment • Loyalty/commitment • Business awareness • Continuous improvement
Work	**Resources** • Workload • Schedules/cycles • Tools/equipment • Data/information • Physical environment	**Methods** • Work processes • Resource allocation • Process monitoring • In-process correction • SOPs	**Products/Services** • Product/service delivery • Customer satisfaction • Quality • Quantity • Service levels

This model serves reasonably (this is not a reassuring word) well as a guide for thinking through all that might be involved in any particular system performance improvement opportunity. It will also serve as a handy organizing tool for data. Without some form of tool to guide broad system thinking it is very easy to overlook areas that might have a bearing on the issue at hand.

Additionally, as with the previous model, this one is also useful for triggering deeper thinking as part of an interview or focused group process. This model can be used with interviews or groups much in the same way the previous model can be used, but is often most helpful when dealing with managers or focus groups in the analysis phase.

There is a tendency for individuals or groups, particularly when they are managers or supervisors in the targeted performance area, to in effect "fixate" on some particular aspect of the perceived performance or dysfunction. When this appears to be the case, use of this model can help you break out of this repetitive symptomology.

It takes no more than 2 or 3 minutes to explain the grid, and you can then point out that all the discussion to that point has focused on one particular box or few boxes. You then cross out that box or boxes and ask the interviewee or focus group attendees to leave the crossed out area(s) and address the remaining areas to see if they can uncover any relevant issues in any of them.

Third is the process or approach that is a bit more complex— the focus group. As was stated earlier, focus groups are actually a necessary analysis component when the performance under investigation is a group performance. Only group analysis techniques have the reliable property of representing the "group" mindset (which can often be quite distinct from the individual mindset) that is applied to the performance of the job.

However, this technique requires a deep understanding of the advantages and pitfalls of this approach coupled with sufficient experience and training to enable a rigorous application of the proper methods of conducting focus groups.[2] The common problem I have seen is the HPT practitioner engaging in this approach with only a rudimentary understanding of the principles coupled with the mistaken impression that it is a simple process requiring only minimal facilitation skills to use effectively. This is a very wrongheaded, and potentially dangerous, misunderstanding of this technique.

When not done properly and rigorously, this approach can almost guarantee incomplete, and even more dangerous, inaccurate or significantly exaggerated data that will guide the HPT practitioner down a well-intended "garden path" of their own creation. Whether this is a conscious or unconscious act is irrelevant. Your data end up skewed and often far a field from what was required.

It is worth pointing out again that alignment is a basic condition of clarity. If the system is not aligned, you can be assured that the worker, and often the supervisors and managers as well, are getting messages from the "organizational System" that are confusing in the aggregate and clouding the clarity about what is desired and intended.

A common problem when dealing with entire subsystems or enterprise-wide interventions resides in the vertical elements of the organizational structure—moving from the "front line work" up through supervision and into the various levels of management. When analyzing the supervision through management levels, a common troublesome phenomenon is often described as a pattern of people "working" one or two levels lower than they should be working.

When analyzing issues within workgroups, another similar pattern is often described as the group or team working at lower levels of "initiative" or "self-direction" than desired. Empowerment or delegation is often suggested as a central part of the eventual Performance Improvement solution.

You might well be asking yourself right now "What in the world is similar about those two problems?" The answer is that it is about people, at whatever level in the organization, working routinely below the levels of performance than what is desired and required. A relatively simple model of "competence levels" that both identifies the general level of performance and aids in guiding how you raise these general levels of competence can be very useful.

One such model is the Delegation/Empowerment and Initiative Model below.

DELEGATION/EMPOWERMENT MODEL

State of Delegation	Level 1	Level 2	Level 3	Level 4
Manager Role	Identify need	Identify need	Identify need	Identify need
	Define results	Define results	Define results	Define results
	Specify what to do	Specify what to do	Specify what to do	Specify what to do
	Specify how to do it	Specify how to do it	Specify how to do it	Specify how to do it
Staff Role	Do it	Do it	Do it	Do it
Levels of Initiative	Ask for assignment	Suggest, then do	Do, then inform	Do, report periodically

This model potentially has a number of uses, not the least being yet another way to break down elements of a job, much like the Predictability/Time Delay Grid above. In addition, this model is a good representation of one of the ways to successively build levels of competence and initiative—by going one step at a time.

I have found this model particularly useful in resolving both of the generic problems of people working below the levels of performance desired.

Teamwork

Much has been written on teamwork, and I will make no attempt to try to cover that topic here. However, I would be severely remiss if I made no mention of *teamwork* in a book on implementing Performance Improvement initiatives in organizations. Many, many organizational tasks require the work of a team, working in concert to accomplish organizational objectives that could not be completed by an individual working alone. Effective teamwork is one of the basic "givens" when dealing with organizational performance. The ability of groups of people to work together effectively as a cohesive team is central to enabling organizations to successively achieve their purpose. All performance plans that require group cooperation/ interaction must incorporate good teamwork principles. And if effective teamwork is not the norm in the current operations, remediating that situation will most often be one of the critical components of a successful performance intervention.

Now, with all of the above on teamwork said, it must also be pointed out that very cohesive teams can also become a serious problem for an organization.

Most organizations are composed of a number of teams with differing functional and operational responsibilities. It is the combination of all these teams working in alignment that will enable the organization to achieve its goals.

Very strong teams can also very easily become very insular and internally focused. So while effective teamwork is an integral part of organizational effectiveness efforts, so is partnering or teamwork between teams.

Partnering and Teamwork

Organizations require people to work effectively both *within* groups and *between* groups. For example, successful product development requires the efforts of a team, not just creative individuals working in isolation; and bringing the product to the marketplace requires close coordination between engineering and design, marketing, and other groups. In the latter situation, very strong teamwork within teams can actually get in the way.

It can lead to an "us against them" mentality in which teams resist each other's demands and even compete with each other for resources, rewards, or credit. Often a major issue for organizations is building effective *partnering* relationships. Partnering becomes critical when groups or teams with different interests must work together toward mutual goals. Partnering is a way of working interdependently with other groups or organizations that gains maximum benefits for both. Although both partnering and teamwork are interdependent relationships, there are some real differences between the two. Work teams typically have a single overriding mission; in partnering relationships, the overall missions of the groups may be quite different.

There are four key components of partnering: one "what" and three "hows." The "what" of partnering is mutual goals; partnering cannot work unless groups recognize that they have mutual goals. The three "how" requirements are openness, respect, and shared responsibility.

Mutual Goals

Avoiding the destructive "us vs. them" mentality requires that both parties in a potential partnering relationship have mutual goals or interests—and have a clear agreement on what those mutual interests are. For example, vendor-purchaser relationships can become adversarial when vendors see the goal as selling the most product for the highest price or least effort. Purchasers are then encouraged to look at getting as much as they can from the vendor at the best possible terms and do not ethically and practically focus on adding value to all stakeholders.

In reality, both parties have a mutual interest in having the product or service function effectively *and* in seeing that the other gets a good deal financially. Purchasers who help a vendor get a good deal also ensure themselves a healthy, cooperative supplier who can perform well for them and will be likely to put out extra effort. Vendors who help a purchaser get a good and useful deal also ensure themselves a loyal, supportive customer. While this sounds simple and logical, much actual behavior in customer-supplier relationships is adversarial. This happens when one or both parties chooses to focus on areas in which goals are not congruent to the detriment of areas in which they have mutual interests. The partnering principles are designed to help those in partnering relationships emphasize their areas of mutual interest and avoid adversarial behavior.

Potential Problems in Focusing on Mutual Goals

- Differences in goal priorities
- Scarcity of resources—e.g., time, money, personnel
- Many directly competing goals
- Failure to recognize the value of others' contribution to a mutual goal
- Lack of mutual commitment to achieving goals

Positive Practices

- Reconcile goals or compromise on alternatives.
- Remove one or more goals (give up goal).
- Setup agreed guidelines for managing priorities.
- Manage the conflicts as they arise.
- Relate conflicts to overall joint mission and goals.
- Accept validity of both positions—deal with one at a time.
- Expand the partnership to include supporting each other's goals.
- Encourage solving problems at the level at which they occur.

Things to Avoid

- Fighting; active hostility
- Harboring grudges, nurturing resentments, ill feelings
- Protectionism or over-control
- Escalating conflicts
- Ending the relationship (last resort)

Openness

Openness means that both parties in a genuine partnering relationship must feel free to raise any issue or concern and confidently expect that it will be received in a spirit of cooperation. That is, there should be no "sore points" that can't be raised on either side. Nor should the parties be protective of information that is relevant to their mutual goals. A free and open exchange of relevant information is required for partnering to work. Withholding key information usually becomes evident very soon. When it occurs, it creates the impression that the other party is trying to gain an edge—and almost always lends an adversarial note to the relationship.

Potential Problems in Maintaining Openness

- Past antagonism makes it difficult to initiate cooperative discussions.
- People withhold useful or necessary information for personal advantage.
- People are concerned about protection.

Positive Practices

- Prepare an opening in advance; try it out on someone.
- Hold a discussion with a neutral third party present.
- Openly acknowledge past barriers; state desire to forget them.
- Stay open; avoid retaliation if initial attempts are not successful.
- Directly ask for information if it's not volunteered.
- Confront withholding: "We have to have full information to work together."
- If necessary, acknowledge the requirement to protect some information; agree on how to handle it.

Things to Avoid

- Being defensive when addressing questions or concerns
- "One-upmanship" by sharing information in a way intended to gain advantage or leverage

Respect

True respect means behaving toward others in a way that assumes they have value—that differences stem from legitimate motives and that people will typically behave in a responsible way. When differences are respected as legitimate, they can be an energizing force, and a source of innovation and flexibility. Lack of respect for differences can destroy a partnership through mistrust and misunderstanding. Differences among people provide great opportunities for synergy or dysfunction.

Most people want and intend to behave responsibly and competently. When we respect that, and behave accordingly, we are likely to get responsible, competent behavior from others. Yet all too often, management behavior sends signals that indicate lack of respect for people's intentions. For example, when we institute restrictive and overly detailed expense control systems, we signal an expectation that people will not behave responsibly without them; when we give overly detailed instructions for an ordinary task, we may signal an expectation that the person will otherwise make a mess of things.

Potential Problems in Maintaining Respect

- Lack of understanding of others' values and circumstances
- Lack of appreciation for how others see us
- Restrictive organizational systems that signal lack of respect to many
- Reacting to differences in a hostile or defensive manner

Positive Practices

- Behaving in a way that supports the confidence and self-esteem of others
- Resolving issues through problem-solving, rather than giving directives
- Behaving as though you expect others to do things right as well as do what is right; adding value to all stakeholders
- Acting as if you assume differences in view stem from legitimate motives

- Providing direction in the form of guidelines, rather than rules
- Treating irresponsible behavior as an exception, rather than a signal to establish controls or sanctions
- Looking to expand, rather than limit individual decision making
- Asking appropriate questions; taking time to learn cultural differences

Things to Avoid

- Talking about other groups behind their backs
- Treating commitments made as minor, or trivial
- Stereotyping or "labeling" others
- Communicating a low opinion of others' capabilities or contribution
- Taking decisions away from them

Shared Responsibility

An effective partnering relationship requires mutual commitment to goals, decisions, actions, and the consequences of those actions. That means sharing the effort—but more importantly, sharing responsibility for making things work and taking a fair share of the risks when they do not. Partnering relationships will not work if people focus on trying to avoid responsibility or risk. And they will seldom work well if shared responsibility is taken to mean that groups carve out independent roles for themselves—"We'll do our piece, and you do yours."

Successful partnering requires the commitment of all parties to all aspects of the joint effort, even though one may take primary responsibility for implementing a given area. All too often, groups try to control responsibility and risk by finding a limited role that they are comfortable with and by avoiding involvement in the other party's role. In so doing, they limit apparent risk to themselves, but often increase the overall risk of failure of the joint effort.

We can and should limit risk, of course—but we must take risks. Partnering will not work where one party is absolutely free of all risk, or where either party focuses on trying to shift risk to the other.

Potential problems in sharing responsibility and risk

- People fail to treat commitments seriously.
- People have different understandings of "quality."
- One party communicates distrust of the other.
- Overload: one or both parties tend to over-commit.
- One or both parties attempt to over-control; following the rules becomes more important than reaching the goal.
- Imbalance of effort: one party does the work, the other reviews it.
- Protection: one party focuses on ensuring that "we aren't held accountable for your mistakes."

Positive Responses

- Take the time to be clear about agreements.
- Ask for early warning, should problems arise.
- Ensure mutual understanding of the importance of meeting commitments.
- Focus on solutions, rather than blame.
- Review understanding of agreements.
- Work to the spirit, not the letter, of the commitment.
- Focus on principles and guidelines, rather than rules and regulations.

Things to Avoid

- Establishing penalties
- Assuming or expecting the worst (we usually get what we expect)
- Hoarding, rather than sharing, credit
- Using deceit or misdirection to avoid exposing areas of vulnerability
- Apathy; letting the other party take the load when things get difficult

- Showing lack of respect for others' contributions
- Unilateral decisions in areas of mutual responsibility
- Shifting blame to the other party if things go wrong

The principles of partnering provide a basis for building solid working relationships between groups, individuals, or organizations that have different interests, agendas, or objectives—but must, nevertheless, work together to achieve mutual goals. They can be used at the beginning of a relationship to develop clarity and forestall misunderstandings, or at any time, to resolve or prevent problems.

Partnering works. It has resulted in significant improvements in the working relationships between:

- internal departments;
- customers and vendors;
- manufacturers and distributors;
- contractors and sub-contractors;
- parties to a joint venture; and
- unions and management.

And it can produce substantial savings and efficiency gains by reducing duplication of effort, errors and rework, misunderstandings, and "turf" wars.

Heuristics

There is an interesting drive in the evolution of HPT over the past 30 years to try to make everything related to performance quantitative and to ignore qualitative measures, or alter them into some distorted version of another quantitative measure.

A simple example of this comes from the banking industry. For years, the guiding principle and standard mantra in banks when deciding to extend a loan or turn it down were referred to as the "Three Cs of Credit." These three Cs were cash, collateral, and character. "Cash" and "collateral" are relatively easy to quantify, but "character" is far harder. Nowadays in most banks and other financial institutions, the character component has been reduced to a credit score number, and the initial depth and strength of the balanced qualitative and quantitative approach have been lost in most instances.

I remember early in my career I was working at a large financial institution in San Francisco. In the course of doing some internal research, I had discovered the Archives Department. The old gentleman who ran the department showed me the note from which the original loan to Walt Disney was made with which he founded Disney Studios. In the space where the banker was to specify the back-up to justify making the loan, the bank founder, one of the financial radicals of his time, had written in "an honest man with a dream." This was a clear statement of character as the basis for the loan and most clearly a qualitative judgment.

I feel reasonably certain that if a "credit score" had been substituted for the more personal reading of "character," then this loan would have never been made. When we lose the essence of qualitative issues in living systems, we may be losing the center piece of the essence of a living System.

To try to move all measures to those that are quantitative and to attempt to reduce to near zero or eliminate all variability is to move from the living and organic world to the mechanical world in which "humans" do not fit.

Our American drive to egalitarianism has had a side effect that runs directly opposite to what I think were initially intended. Rather than increasing our levels of humanity justice to mankind, we have reduced our condition to one that does not allow for humans to be human.

At the level of creation, all men may well be created equal. But once the process of "living" begins, differentiation begins to assert itself, and differing levels of capability, desire, focus, application, interest, and intellect come in to play. All people do not operate as equals in all things—and the degree of potential variation is quite large. Character, as a statement of probability of certain behaviors occurring or not occurring, cannot be reduced to a set of numbers. Variability cannot be engineered out of the system.

Behavioral predictability in humans cannot be reduced to an absolute in each and every case. Behavioral predictability in humans cannot be specified and controlled to the operant level.

Precise cloning of behavior will only work in relation to robots, not humans. Again, when the cogs in the System are sentient, some degree of variability is a given. This degree of variability must be "built in" and allowed to achieve maximum performance with humans. To eliminate the subtle variations of behavior is to eliminate the humanity.

What is required are viable "guiding principles," not cookbooks with set lists, or algorithms, about how to accomplish each and every task. One of the most viable tools to achieve this are statements of "behavioral practice" or practices, rather than specific behaviors.

For example, when training clerks to work in a 7-Eleven store, the company or franchisee would like customers to leave the store with the feeling that their business, and future business, is appreciated. A traditional "cookbook" approach is to teach and require the clerk to end each transaction with the words "Thank you for shopping at 7-Eleven. Please come again." This phrase then becomes a rote mantra and is stripped of its "feeling" and no longer conveys anything but compliance to a requirement that now has nothing to do with how the clerk actually feels about the transaction. And worse, it no longer conveys anything to the customer beyond mechanical obedience on the part of the clerk and often becomes the target of derision.

On the other hand, a simple heuristic in the form of a behavioral practice allows for "human" variation that equally allows for maintaining some degree of human feeling. The behavioral practice would read, "Behave in a manner that conveys to the customer that you appreciate their business." This is a heuristic; a guideline for behavior—it focuses on the desired result or impact *on the customer.* All too often the drive for cookbooks rather than heuristics comes from focusing on the observable behavior of the performer rather then the impact on the receiving system (the customer).

A great deal of the time in managing performance, we are focusing on actions that are critical to results, but the results are the impact on the receiving system, not the specific behavior exhibited by the performer.

This is the core of most training and job aids focused on management and supervision. The receiving system of management and supervisory actions are the workers. If the humanity of the message is lost by reducing it to the level of rote recall and the emotionless mechanical applications of words and processes, it will have little impact of a positive nature and may well become the subject of distrust and discomfort. Distrust and discomfort in the working relationships in an organization are not a path to high levels of productivity and efficiency.

Clarity of intent is often more important than detailed specifics of what to do. Heuristics often begin with statements of the desired result of the performance, and this is followed by what are usually a series of "indicators" of a positive or negative nature that will help guide the performance without dictating any one set path to successful conclusion. Indicators may include such things as examples and non-examples, a simple list of positive indicators and negative indicators, and things to "watch" for of both a positive and negative nature. An example of guidance materials of this sort can be found in the section above on Partnering.

Time and Priorities

Another common problem I have seen in performance interventions is a curious absence of any sense of reality in regard to time and the relationship of time and priority setting. I have yet to do work in an organization where people generally report that they have sufficient time to accomplish all their tasks each and every day. In fact it is common for people to report, particularly managers and supervisors, that "no one gets everything done each day."

Ensuring Clarity and Ability requires people to have the time to accomplish a task. One of the key aspects of "having time" means clarity on the relative priority of any given task when compared to any other tasks the performer may have on his or her plate. All too often the *relative* importance/priority of any particular activity in relation to other tasks that may compete for available time is not clear.

Consequences for failure are often built in to performance interventions as part of the plan to ensure performance. However, all too often this is done in isolation from the rest of the performance system and even the rest of the individual job, and if not done with the *total* job in mind, the intervention can result in creating a misalignment problem by inappropriately increasing focus and drive on only one aspect of the overall job.

Culture and Peer Expectations

One last comment on Clarity and Ability: The cultural norms (acceptable behavioral/social patterns) in the organization are a critical aspect of Clarity and Ability. In HPT, we all too often resort to thinking about things like Clarity and Ability only in terms of the individual performer and not the "group" aspects of performance. Peer expectations and interaction can have as much impact on Clarity and Ability to perform as anything else and must always be considered in the overall performance design. And of course, this is particularly true when dealing with group-based performances.

Endnotes

1. Including internal and external consequences.

2. A good short article on conducting focus groups can be found at http://www.managementhelp.org/evaluatn/focusgrp.htm. Also see listing under references in this of this chapter.

Chapter 6
Achieving Sustained Results

In what should be a statement of the obvious, let me point out that the purpose of most changes and most Performance Improvement projects is to achieve *sustained* useful and positive results over time.

Years of endeavors and follow-up on attempts to change how things are done in organizations have demonstrated that as difficult as it is to achieve any measurable change in organizational processes and results, short-term, or momentary, changes are far easier to deliver than is sustained long-term change.

At a very high level, the issue of sustainability is a simple proposition. This issue was dealt with in the first chapter of this book. Sustainability is about how well the "solution," or new way of working, is aligned within the overall *System*[1] and adds value at all levels—organizational and societal. However, as was covered in the first chapter, while conceptually simple, the actual activities of getting an organizational system aligned, and then maintaining that alignment, can be a very complex and consuming task. In terms of a living system (which is what you have when people are involved in the system), it is a continual challenge. To repeat a comment from earlier in this book—any organization composed of more than seven people is dysfunctional by definition. Competitive edge is about being less dysfunctional than your competitors (as you move from dysfunctional to functional).

Making people aware of what is desired and ensuring that they have the ability to perform as desired is the enabler to achieving the "holy grail" of HPT, which is a sustained desired and valuable result. There are a number of factors involved in achieving this end result, and these include the following:

- The ability of the target population to measure and track their own progress

- Support subsystems, including incentives and rewards, that make it easier to change than not change

- Supportive actions on the part of those "around" the target population

- The target staff believing in the value and importance of performing as desired
  - The "social" group believing in the value/importance
  - The observed consequences of changing and not changing
- Support and follow-through by immediate supervision
- The value placed on the change by the organization and how it signals that value

It is also important that the "results" of a systemic HPT plan have two types of measurable results—otherwise the result is not systemic and potential success is seriously jeopardized, particularly in organizational settings. The best *complete* definition of "results" I have seen is embedded in a quote from William Pasmore, one of the founding fathers of Socieotechnical Systems:

Effective organizations are those which deliver excellent results by any measure of cost, quality, or efficiency, while simultaneously enhancing the energy and commitment of the members of the organization to the success of the enterprise.

This quotation provides another way of thinking about results, particularly in the organizational context. Any performance plan—be it aimed at an individual, a group of individuals, a team, a group of teams, or an entire organization—should have built into it two primary properties, both of which can be measured:

- It should result in measurable improvements in some measure or measures of cost, quality, effectiveness, and efficiency.

- It should measurably improve the energy and commitment of the people involved to the success of the enterprise.

If the performance plan does not deliver *both* it is not systemic, and sustained impact becomes highly questionable.

Evaluation

One of the key sources of data to adjust and maintain performance intervention results is evaluation studies. Unfortunately, all too many evaluation studies do not produce actionable data, particularly in the case of systemic organizational interventions. Often the problem with the data is that it focuses solely on the end result with no attention to the intermediate enablers that had to be in place to allow the final results to occur; there are no "en-route" results that are evaluated and thus it is difficult to tell where problems come from at the end of a program or project.

The point has to be made that being useful and provide actionable data evaluation, particularly in relation to more complex interventions, can get a bit difficult—and elements of it *may* not focus on what we would normally call "results." In the literature of Performance Improvement, this is often termed "formative evaluation."

Most larger-scale interventions have multiple parts to them, and often some of these early parts may in reality be only "enablers" to later parts that actually deliver the desired result. This does not mean you should forgo some form or level of evaluation of those early part or parts; it just means your "result" is more limited and will not reflect the "actual" end-of-project result you are heading toward. I call these "en-route results," and that is why I use the three levels of results: Mega, Macro, and Micro (Kaufman, 2006).[2]

For example, W. Edwards Deming, one of the founders of the modern quality movement and a principal proponent of statistical process control, got very adamant in his later years about the "must haves" that preceded effective quality management. He would make the point very strongly that any company that initiated a quality program with "targets, objectives, and numbers" was foredoomed to failure!

Quite obviously targets, goals, and numbers are at the heart of statistical process control, which is generally considered to be a critical component of any quality System. Dr. Deming was not backing away from statistical measures, he was simply trying to strongly make the point that there were some other things that came first, and if they were not done, no amount of *measurement* would resolve the quality problems. I think he was also objecting to silly indicators. I would add that all indicators—results, targets, and objectives—must be derived from a needs (not "wants") assessment and link all three levels of results and consequences.

The point here is that many complex or "higher order" processes and procedures in organizations are the result of a series of *interdependent* activities, some of which are required precursors. There is no inherent perceived "value" in quality measures, providing those measures will not have an impact because the metrics will be ignored. Equally, having the "value" without measures to manage and track quality will not deliver the required desired final results. So, in terms of an intervention, first the value has to be established, and then the means to manage and track the desired result can be put in place. Only when the value was in place in the organization would measures have an impact.

In other words, if people thought other things were more important than quality, measuring the quality would not have any impact. So, first get the conviction in place and then make sure the organizational culture puts a high value on quality,[3] and at that point, measurement systems will have a distinct impact on what is produced.

On a recent project to re-establish the Department of Justice in an East European country after years of communist bureaucracy, it became evident very early in the process that the incumbents in the jobs had no concept of a court and legal system that was intended to serve the "needs[4] of the citizens". Their history had always been one of serving the "needs" of the government and the party—the citizens were secondary.

Even though in the end this project would be measured by impact and value in the eyes of the citizenry, the starting point had to be getting a basic belief System in place with all the employees that the fundamental purpose of a "rule of law" had to center on service to the citizenry. *Then* the processes and measures could be crafted and tracked on the targeted end result.

Generally speaking, an evaluation effort would not focus on belief or understanding—which is far too soft and not what we would normally call "results." Yet, if we did not make certain that the belief system was in place, we could easily proceed with the later parts of the change effort, have them fail, and then wonder why it did not deliver what it was supposed to deliver. As has been stated repeatedly in this book, many, and possibly most, systemic organizational Performance Improvement projects are both iterative in nature and have multiple pieces to them that have to all come together to achieve the desired end result. Evaluation in these types of projects, particularly when a primary purpose of the evaluation is to refine and solidify the results, is all too often not a simple and straightforward measurement of the final outputs and outcomes.[5] The final output is the result of a series of interlocking and interdependent parts of the system being aligned to deliver the final output and useful outcomes.

Make sure that your evaluation efforts include measures of necessary precursors such that you can refine and adjust the overall systemic nature of the intervention, and a focus on the end result alone will not deliver this type of information.[6]

In addition to evaluation, there are a few other general concepts that can have broad and systemic impact that will underpin much of any systemic change effort, and it is the system and its interactions that will deliver the results or not.

The Energy Investment Model

A primary generic issue around successful change that has been referenced a number of times in this book is when the performance in question is a group-based, or multiple-group-based, performance. In these situations, success hinges on getting the *group* aligned in active support of the change and the purposes of change. People influence one another, especially in regard to group activities. Humans are social animals, and organizations are in effect small (or large) communities. The Energy Investment Model (EIM) is one of the most useful tools I have found for addressing the issue of commitment on both an individual *and* a group level. This model is also helpful in evaluation and in ongoing measurement and reinforcement of the overall effort.

This model was created by a former business partner, Claude Lineberry. We were well into the transformation at British Airways and experiencing the normal ups and downs of group sessions, trying to instill a new set of values and methods of managing the business. Claude was puzzling over the varying responses we got from different groups and, during the course of a flight from London to San Francisco, ended up jotting down this model that seemed to capture a lot of what was going on. Since then, the model has been used in multiple programs around the world with great success in building commitment to the change and in follow-up activities—particularly with management—designed to solidify and embed the change into the normal operating patterns.

Achieving short-term behavior change as the result of a seminar, workshop or training session is comparatively easy. Similarly, gaining verbal acceptance and endorsement of a strategic or operational plan is not difficult. Transferring that initial change or acceptance into sustained on-the-job behavior over a longer time period, however, can prove extremely difficult if not impossible.

A multitude of reasons have been put forward for this phenomenon, particularly job pressure, lack of support from management, and/or lack of incentive. While these obviously influence on-the-job performance, it is rare that they are fully accountable for the lack of change in performance. It seems that a substantial number of people—despite the insights gained from the workshop, meeting, or plan, and their initial commitment—choose to do little differently on the job over a longer period of time.

The Energy-Attitude Dynamic

If we look at the distribution of people in an organization, it appears that they fall into four organizational groups or communities, defined by the *attitude* they hold about the organization and the *level of energy* that they choose to invest in doing their job.

The interrelationship of the *attitude* and *energy* dynamics to define these organizational communities is shown below.

The Energy Investment Model

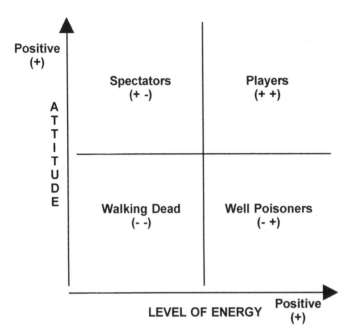

The four communities are:

- **Walking Dead** (*Low Energy—Negative Attitude*): These people feel powerless to take action or influence events. Typically, they have been punished for mistakes, not empowered, and micromanaged—never fully engaged as a part of the organization. They "just do the job," provide little else in the form of ideas or effort, and wait for the change to go away or for their retirement date to arrive.

- **Spectators** (*Low Energy—Positive Attitude*): Spectators are long on verbal endorsement and short on performance supporting the change. They have a history that has caused them to be risk-averse, choosing not to act until it is clear that the action is safe. In times of organizational turbulence, especially downsizing or consolidation, a surprising number of managers who feel threatened choose to reside in the relatively safe Spectator community.

- **Well Poisoners** *(High Energy—Negative Attitude)*: Well Poisoners are often highly articulate, good technical performers who are extremely angry at the organization for any of a number of reasons. This negative attitude, coupled with high energy, takes the form of damning the organization's past and dooming its future. The focus of their "well poisoning" is often the organization's leadership and management, or its proposed plans and initiatives. Left unchecked, that can become organizational saboteurs.

- **Players** *(High Energy—Positive Attitude)*: These are the people who make things happen in any organization. They tend to hold a realistic and generally optimistic view of the organization's situation and its future, coupled with a willingness to put extra effort and energy into the organization's improvement and success. They can, however, be overloaded to the point of frustration or failure because of their willingness and desire to make things better.

The point of **The Energy Investment Model** is not to label people in the organization by identifying the group or community to which they belong. In fact, everyone finds themselves—at least occasionally—in each of the communities. The point is that it is the leadership and management of the organization that direct individuals to reside in a particular group or community.

The leadership and management practices demonstrated to the organization's people are the prime determinants of the attitude that they hold about the organization and the level of energy that they are willing to invest in doing their jobs.

No organization knowingly and actively recruits and hires Walking Dead, Spectators, or Well Poisoners. Almost everyone takes a job because they feel good about the company they are joining and want to succeed in the job—almost all enter the organization in the Player community. How the organization treats them, and especially how the leadership and management of the organization functions, directs them to either remain in the Player community or take up residence in one of the three less-desirable communities.

Where do you live?

Asking yourself in which community you, as a leader and manager, reside most of the time is a very valuable activity. Where do you think you reside—Walking Dead, Spectator, Well Poisoner, or Player? More importantly, if you are a supervisor or manager, where do those who report to you think you reside? I have often used the Energy Investment Model in my work with organizations and have actually asked leaders and managers to place themselves in one of the quadrants of the model and then asked their direct reports to place them on the model. In our experience, more often than not the leaders and managers have a more optimistic self-perception than the perceptions of those who report to them.

The Energy Investment Model is a useful template for leaders and managers to use in thinking about the demographics of their team or department or the organization as a whole. What percentage of people are perceived to reside in each of the four communities? How can they best be redirected and moved from the Walking Dead, Spectator, or Well Poisoner community to the Player community?

This may provide valuable insight regarding perceived resistance to organizational change or the pace of that change and to the perceptions that current leadership and management practices are creating in the organization's people.

It is good to remember a tried and true maxim of organizational change: To get people to where you want them to be, you must first know where they are. The Energy Investment Model is a diagnostic tool to help you understand the organizational communities in which people reside, and how their residence can cause them to either support and participate in organizational change, or resist and work against it.

Without a doubt, one of the most powerful forces for sustained change is the collective view and opinion of the people who make up the organization. When the mass of the people are in support of the new manner of working, it tends to have long-term sustainability. And you will hopefully have noted the wording "*mass* of the people are in support." Organizational effectiveness and management effectiveness are not an issue of getting 100% of the people in full support (although that would be nice). It is about getting the bulk of the people in support so that the organizational norms drive acceptance and support of the organizational goals.

Sustainability and Management/Leadership

A second generic issue around the topic of change and sustainability is the management and leadership being brought to bear both on the overall organization and on the solution and its various elements.

As was covered in Chapter 2 when the alignment model was discussed, the routine behaviors of the supervisors and managers that are visible to the target population are a major source of direction, both overt and covert. Getting managers aware of how they are perceived, and even better getting them to consciously *manage* how they are perceived, is one of the most critical aspects of effective management.

Tools like employee satisfaction surveys and 360° feedback surveys are fairly common tactics utilized in attempts to make managers more aware of the impact they are having on the people they are responsible for managing. A proper and powerful use of 360° feedback surveys was discussed in Chapter 2 on Alignment.

In larger systems, the more difficult issue of management awareness is in getting the top management group aware of the impact they are having multiple layers down and across the organization. Traditional methodologies, such as employee surveys and 360° feedback surveys, lose much of their punch when dealing with the senior team of a large organization. At this level, executives are all too aware of the relative uniqueness of their part of the organization from all other parts, and are generally operating all too far away from the daily reality of operations.

The primary issue with senior executives is to make sure the data are totally personalized to that executive yet tied directly to the organizational intent of the company. The best way to get the support of senior executives in larger organizations, particularly when you are having to work cross functionally, is to develop a position of "informed self-interest" in each of the senior executives.

One of the best tools I have seen for accomplishing this awareness with top management groups is a technique some of us have dubbed the Management Mirror. As I know of, there is no other method with as much chance of overall positive impact on a senior team and their ability to consciously and effectively impact the results of the organization. Let's see just how this process is done.

The Management Mirror

The Management Mirror is a highly effective process for conducting an in-depth senior management analysis "to take a look in the mirror" as it were—and truly see the effect the senior team has on the organization, both individually and collectively.

This is a fundamentally qualitative process to specify the impact of the senior management team on organizational processes and behavior. It delves into the questions "How is the senior team perceived, individually and collectively?" and "What impact do these perceptions have regarding how people behave down, through, and across the organization?"

These perceptions have a lot to do with how patterns are set for the way business is done as an organization. This approach goes *far* beyond the standard 360° feedback process. This approach requires individual interviews with each direct report of the executive team, and direct interviews with each of the direct reports of these direct reports. There are focus groups going on down further into the organization, but for all interviews and focus groups, the topic of exploration is the senior team and how they are perceived individually and collectively. What are the perceived hot buttons, views, biases and prejudices, preferences, likes and dislikes, expectations and demands both overt and covert?

Further, the process uncovers not only overt demands/ expectations that have been specifically requested in writing or speaking, but also (and I would argue even more importantly) perceived demands/wants/expectations.

Managers, and particularly the executive group, have a tendency to think that what they specifically ask for or request are the only critical aspects of their daily performance in terms of organizational results. However, there is often more effective direction to the troops from the off-hand remark or even nonverbal response than from the formal pronouncements. The executive group in particular must become far more conscious of their overt and covert impact on others and must realize that all their behavior, both observed and assumed, is sending messages for which they must be accountable.

This overall process allows no place to hide. The individual data for each senior team member is shared with the rest of the team, including the CEO's data. It is by definition comprehensive, detailed, and personal, *sometimes* disturbing, and *always* highly effective. A common statement by participants when this activity is completed is: "This is the single most beneficial thing that I have ever done in my career."

The Management Mirror, unlike prepackaged surveys and assessments, does not force fit the data or the questions asked in a standard or fixed approach. It is a process, not a product, and as such, is customized to each organization that employs it. It does not assume everyone is doing the same things. It does not assume all executives are supposed to act in one particular style or way. It responds to the individual styles and business priorities of each member of the senior team and reflects the impact of this behavior on the ability of the rest of the organization to accomplish the organization's strategic goals.

Through individual interviews with the CEO, all of his or her reports, all of their direct reports, skip level sampling interviews and focus groups further down in the organization, the information collected forms an extremely accurate picture of how the behaviors of individual executives and the senior team as a whole are perceived. It then goes on to detail the impact these perceptions have on the performance of others. The Management Mirror reflects how effectively the organizational strategy and business priorities of senior management are communicated by them to the organization's people and how their individual and team behavior facilitates or impedes achieving desired results. In essence, the Management Mirror focuses on the fact that management behavior at the top of the organization is about direction, motivation, guidance, and influence, and not about the planning, supervising, and allocation of resources associated with middle management. Two examples of real Management Mirror reports (sanitized to protect the individuals and company) are included as Appendix A. One is a report about the CEO, and the other is about a direct report to the CEO. There is uniqueness about senior management. It is very different at the top. For executives, individual behavior has a ripple effect throughout the organization that goes far beyond themselves. Simple requests, casual inquiries, or even routine day-to-day behavior of senior management can have significant and often unintended impact on other parts of the organization without the senior manager ever being aware.

As an example, the operations manager of an international freight company, a man of high energy and strong opinion, had the habit of pointing his index finger at the person to whom he was talking to emphasize his point. Since the rest of his hand was closed, it appeared as if he was shooting the person with an imaginary pistol. Some found this humorous, but most saw it as aggressive and angry. All found it disconcerting. The operations manager was totally unaware of this behavior and its impact on others.

Members of the organization will often ascribe characteristics or priorities to the position and not the person currently in the position. Executive wants, needs (gaps in results), and business priorities are subject to interpretation—and often misinterpretation. This impact can resonate and dramatically affect business results, for better or for worse. Middle managers will drive things that they think an executive wants.

Additionally, the higher a person rises in an organization, the less likely he or she will have access to unfiltered information about his or her behavior and its impact on organizational performance. Many subordinates are hesitant to voice views or opinions candidly and honestly that they feel their boss may not like to hear. When information is passed on, it is often done so delicately that the message is not heard, especially when the information is about the manager's or senior team's behavior.

To illustrate this phenomenon, in a focus group at an automotive frame plant near Detroit, a frustrated supervisor summed it up in these words: "We tell them that a new policy or procedure is pure horse**** for us down here who have to implement it, but by the time the message gets to the guys at the top, they think we called it chocolate pudding!"

The Senior Team as a Team

Management at the top is a collective enterprise. The fact that a senior team or group exists at all is proof that it takes a number of people working together to deliver the shared, agreed-on, and useful results for large organizations. All too often, these teams are teams in name only. Senior executives are often unwilling to become team players. They fight for and defend their own turf and work their own political agendas, often forgetting that executives at this level have two hats to wear. The first, which almost all understand, is the functional hat—dealing with and championing their department or division. The second is that of being a business advisor to the CEO for the whole organization. They must have the ability to rise above the particular function they may be responsible for and advise the CEO about the overall well-being of the total organization. The functional role often overshadows the successful fulfillment of the business advisor role, and the organization suffers.

This phenomenon alone may well account for a large number of failures of systemic cross-functional Performance Improvement efforts.

The rank and file of an organization observes how the top people behave. Individual and group behaviors exhibited by members of the senior or executive team are subject to interpretation, and a variety of perceptions are made and conclusions drawn. One senior manager's behavior can call into question the judgment and effectiveness of the whole senior team. Questions arise around how much commitment there can be in a senior management team that allows one of its members to behave inappropriately, or manage ineffectively, or ignore the impact of their part of the organization on others. If the senior executives don't seem to care about the company, why should anyone else? Top managers who are not perceived to be consistent in word and deed about the leadership and management of the entire organization contribute disproportionately to the inability of the organization to achieve required business results.

How the Management Mirror Works—
First Steps in the Methodology

Before the process even begins, it is imperative that the CEO brief each of his or her team as to the purpose of the Management Mirror. There are no secrets. There are no hidden agendas. The purpose of this intensive and contentious effort is to make senior management fully and totally aware of how their behavior, individually and collectively, impacts the organization and the results it achieves.

The creation of the Management Mirror was prompted by one of my clients, the managing director of a major airline subsidiary, who read an article in the *Financial Times* reporting on a study of senior team perceptions of themselves contrasted with the perceptions of those working for them, including the line "most senior teams would benefit from taking a close look in the mirror before blaming those below them for the company's problems." He faxed the article to me with a handwritten note in the margin asking if our firm could help him and his team take such a look and, as a result, the Management Mirror process was developed.

The Seven-Step Management Mirror Process. The Management Mirror is a seven-step process beginning with in-depth interviews with the CEO, each senior team member who reports to the CEO, and each team member's direct reports. To this basic one-on-one interview process, focus groups or core samples are added with representative groups from all company functions. In this way, the Management Mirror gathers data from 100 percent of the CEO's direct reports, 100 percent of their direct reports, and focus group samples further down in the organization. Data gathered is very thorough, current, and focused on key business issues.

The opening two- or three-hour interview captures the CEO's views on the business as a whole—the strategy, the direction, the priorities—and why they are where they are. Particular focus is on how he or she wants to accomplish the strategies—potential markets, targets, and internal emphasis. The CEO then examines how each function relates to the overall strategy and what role each function plays in the grand plan.

Once the current business situation is covered, the interview shifts to gathering information about those executives responsible for carrying out the business—those who report to the CEO. The CEO is then asked about personal views/perceptions of each fellow executive as head of a particular function or process. Questions examine the reporting relationship, relationship with peers, relative contribution to the management team, and individual leadership and management behaviors.

Finally, the interview ends with the CEO describing his or her view of the senior team *as a team*. Discussing the business situation first and relating all questions to the accomplishment of the strategy provide a very business-focused response. The CEO is forced to think about the team and its members as he or she relates to the current situation and key business issues, with any personal characteristics or commentary secondary to the business requirements both within the organization and outside.

The next phase of the data gathering is to conduct interviews with each of the senior team executives. There are four general parts to these interviews:

1. Gathering perceptions of the CEO's and his or her priorities

2. Gathering perceptions of the senior executive's own function or process and its relationship to the strategy

3. Gathering the senior executive's views of the other functions

4. Gathering views of the senior team, collectively and individually

Specific questions used to gather information may include the following:

- What is it like to work for the CEO?
- What is he/she like as a boss? Strengths? Weaknesses? Relationship to customers?
- What do you have to do to be on the CEO's "good side"?
- What advice do you have for the CEO?
- How is your function aligned with strategy?
- What are YOUR priorities?
- How do you view the other individual contributors? Strengths? Weaknesses?
- Advice for anybody?
- What are the dynamics of the senior team? Internal issues? Working or not?

These interviews usually last one and a half to two hours and reveal a great deal of the inner workings and dynamics of the top team. A common comment at the end of these interviews is "We really covered everything. You didn't leave anything out!"

These interviews continue with all the direct reports of the top team members. Many of the same kinds of questions are used relating to the CEO and their own manager, as well as their perception of their own function and how it ties to the strategy. Specific questions may be asked pertaining to current key issues: How is *quality* defined in your function? Who is the customer in your function? What does your manager expect of you and your function? These "skip level" interviews also allow for comments on all the other senior team members (with whom they have work experience) including their strengths and weaknesses.

The final part of the data gathering is to conduct focus groups on down through the organization. Focus groups consist of 12 to 15 people plus two consultants. A focus group is effectively a discussion group focused on some particular topic or topics, in this case focused on senior management. It takes two consultants to run a focus group: one to keep the dialogue going and ensure that all the people are taking part (facilitating the session) and the other to capture all that is said in comprehensive notes. The number of focus groups per functional area depends entirely on the complexity of each function. Data has to be gathered from each function to accurately represent all of their primary business activities and linkages to external value added.

The focus groups get more into day-to-day activities. Priorities of management get as much attention as in previous interviews, but the question now is to ascertain what management is doing that helps or hinders daily routine. It is here that we often find incredible amounts of time and manpower being spent, supposedly at the behest of senior management, which has little or no impact on the accomplishment of the business strategy.

A poignant example: the new CEO of a global airline soon gained a reputation for his amazing ability to understand and retain enormous amounts of detail about all aspects of daily operations. At his weekly senior team meetings, he would ask very specific and detailed questions of the members of his senior team such as "Tony, Flight 555 to Sidney was short three meals in business class on Tuesday. Why did this happen and what have you done to make sure our flights are properly catered?"

Usually, the queried manager could not answer on the spot—or attempted a vague answer that was rejected as unacceptable by the CEO. This resulted in members of the senior team and their staff spending part of Wednesday and most of Thursday in preparation for the anticipated Friday morning meeting with the CEO, which was known as "The Inquisition."

When, in conjunction with a Management Mirror intervention, the CEO was told about the hundreds of hours that went into preparation for his weekly meeting, he was shocked. At the start of the next meeting, he announced that he was aware of what had been happening and wanted it stopped. "It is clear to me that not everyone has the thirst for detail that I do," he said. "I don't expect you to. I expect you to run your functions effectively, and I will no longer expect answers on the spot. What I do expect is for you to go to the people on your staff and get back to me with an answer to my question as soon as possible."

The CEO got his specific answers in a more reasonable time frame, hundreds of staff hours were recovered, and the dynamic of the Friday meeting changed, moving to a more strategic level. Discussion questions include such things as what they do, their wants, needs, and comments on the competition, who they feel their customer is, what do their customers want/require, and how top team priorities translate into day-to-day activities. The focus groups tell us how the business really works and get to what the rank and file believes about the organization, the management and the business itself and how this impacts what they do on a daily basis.

Next Steps

Once collected, the data have to be analyzed. Some quantitative techniques are applied to analyze the content of the interviews, such as frequency counts or calculation of mean scores on focused surveys or Likert scales around some specific aspect of management. But most of the analysis focuses on the qualitative data. The essence of the Mirror is that it must be upfront and personally relevant—and vast arrays of numbers and computations detract from the powerful, personal nature of the messages and allow for "creative reinterpretation."

The CEO receives a detailed debrief on how he or she is perceived by the next three levels of management—the messages he or she is sending (both intended and unintended—overt and covert) with information on the consequences—and what happens as a result of these perceptions. The consultant and the CEO discuss the relationships between the intention, the actual behavior, the impact, and the strategy. This discussion culminates in an understanding of the desired impact of the CEO's behavior and how to best proceed in getting there. During this meeting, the consultant and the CEO additionally review results of the data gathering for all other members of the senior team.

Detailed debriefs then follow for each of the senior team members. These follow the same format as for the CEO in examining the impact of their individual behavior. In neither case is a written report handed to the CEO or senior team member at this point—that comes later. The intent at this time is to achieve maximum understanding of the gathered information. A verbal report with the executive taking personal notes provides more focus on listening and understanding rather than defending, explaining, or otherwise avoiding the message. The executive must fully understand what the data are showing about how people are reacting to him or her. Good, bad, or indifferent, based on fact, falsity, or interpretation, the people's perceptions are what they are and impact their behavior. The perceptions and resulting behavior have to be understood and managed for the overall good of the organization.

The consultant provides the context for the statements made and conclusions drawn about the executive by those reporting to him or her. The context includes the atmosphere, the tone, the way in which the statements were said, examples, and how it may have been related to other statements. The consultant doing any debrief will have personally completed at least half of the interviews for that particular senior team member. The executive, by his or her very nature, confronts the consultant on the data many times during this process, and the consultant must be thoroughly knowledgeable and confident in the data.

When my colleagues and I engage in these debriefs, we often utilize the fine art of the blunt statement and challenge. If the executive continues to play down or deny any of the information, the volume of delivery is not increased, but the bluntness and level of challenge are, as in, "All ten of your direct reports participated in the Management Mirror, and six of them think you're a jerk (and here's why), three think you're doing OK, and one refused to answer." While this is not a process built for comfort, it *is* built for unequivocal clarity. It is not necessary for the senior manager receiving the feedback to like it, but it is necessary for him or her to understand it and the business consequences that result from it.

The Individual Feedback Report

The Individual Feedback Report is delivered to the senior manager a day or so after the verbal debrief and contains an overall written summary of what was discussed. It serves as a general review, a check on his or her own notes, and is a copy of the report that the CEO has received about him or her. It includes a narrative description of him or her as a leader/manager as perceived by those below him or her, and information as to how effectively he or she communicates messages on various aspects of the tactics such as quality, customer focus, or product development. The emphasis is on day-to-day behavior, the perceptions that he or she creates, and the resulting impact on the work performance of others.

A couple of excerpts describe the tone and feel of the feedback report:

Your Priorities (for the CEO)—

When asked what your top three to five priorities are, your 13 direct reports generated a widely divergent list of 28 different items. A total of 10 different items were given the number one position. Ten different items were also in the number two spot, including seven different from the first 10. The number three spot generated another five additional items. This is a long way of saying that you effectively have no team agreement on priorities.

When asked what animal your behavior suggests to your direct reports, the following menagerie was reported:

- Definitely *not* a bunny

- Rhino (strong, thick skinned, shortsighted, nervous, provokable)

- Vicious dog (might lie quietly, might attack)

- Cape buffalo (aggressive, can show compassion by backing off from the kill)

- Lion (loud roar, unpredictably aggressive)

- Elephant (capable of wreaking havoc without knowing it, intelligent, family oriented, kind)

The flavor of the Individual Feedback Report is very different from what executives encounter in other management surveys or 360° feedback reports and much harder to deny. The language is direct, clear, focused on performance and the business, and data based. Given the scope and thoroughness of the data gathering, it is also wholly irrefutable and intensely personal. The perceptions reported are the current perceived reality; the only questions remaining are how to change those perceptions where they do not aid in the achievement of desired organizational results.

The Event

After all the debriefing interviews have taken place, a meeting is scheduled for the entire senior team. This is recommended as an off-site meeting over two and a half days or more depending on the organization, size of the team, and what issues may be evident. This senior team event has specific components required for its success.

It begins with a Business Brief; the CEO discusses the current situation—the state of the business itself. Setting a business atmosphere focuses the team and creates a touchstone for what follows. The CEO then shares the results of his or her individual data with the rest of the top team. It is important that nothing be left out that is to be presented—warts and all. Some advanced coaching may be required to ensure that the CEO's brief is an effective model, setting the tone for the rest of the team. After one particularly effective presentation by a CEO, a senior manager quipped, "Now we have to follow that?!"

Each of the senior team members follows in turn sharing individual data, asking for help, giving suggestions to others, providing input, and most importantly, talking about his or her data in relationship to the overall business situation. Nothing is hidden and all the information is on the table. The consultants who did the interviews and debriefs are present to ensure that nothing is left out. All the energy that the executives previously expended in posturing or trying to keep things hidden is no longer appropriate. This team event, spanning several days, forces a level of openness and disclosure that many top executives have never experienced. Each individual senior manager builds an action plan as to what to do in terms of changing the way he or she is perceived, and the impact that current perceptions are having on the organization. The group comes to consensus on desired senior team mission, vision, values, norms, and acceptable and unacceptable behaviors; how they will support and challenge one another; and how they will call each other on violations of agreed-upon behavioral contracts. The behavioral contract incorporates team and individual issues. A final Business Brief answers the question of how the results of the Management Mirror analysis tie to the overall business.

The final two steps of the Management Mirror include conducting a follow-up review of individual and team performance monthly for the first three to six months after the team event and conducting a focused follow-up Management Mirror a year later to check on progress, recalibrate, and take corrective action as required.

Causes for Failure

The Management Mirror is a provocative but highly effective method of getting senior executives to sit up and take notice of messages about their behavior. The Management Mirror requires the full support and commitment of the CEO or equivalent top executive if done at a divisional or functional level. Without this full and visible support, the effort will likely fail.

The senior team must be ready for a Management Mirror. The team and its members must be aware of and hopefully frustrated by the knowledge and misgivings that things aren't as they should be. The business situation must be sufficiently challenging so that the team and its members are concerned and willing to try to improve things. They must have worked together long enough to have a behavioral history with one another. Without an appropriate level of readiness, the Management Mirror will not only fail, but may well make the situation worse in terms of senior team development.

Some Caveats

It must be pointed out that the Management Mirror often results in one or more members of the team in a new assignment or leaving the organization. The results of the Management Mirror impact the composition and membership of the team, relative effectiveness of individual team members, and their relationships with others on the team as well as their direct reports. The Management Mirror is most useful when done with intact teams that have been together for a year or more. Each team member requires experience with the others to provide the best observations on behavior. Trust, understanding, and interdependency build from that baseline experience of working together during the senior team meeting and are often one of the first important steps in building the kind of trust and interdependency characteristic of high-performing senior teams.

This is not usually an activity to be undertaken by internal personnel. It is extremely difficult for internal people to solicit the kind of candid information necessary for the Management Mirror process. Internal people are part of the organization and therefore are subject to the organization's biases, beliefs, and political process, making subjectivity in collecting, analyzing, and reporting the data almost impossible. Additionally, the information gathered throughout this process is powerful, highly personal, and often just plain uncomfortable to hear. It is not something that an executive wants shared with internal people.

However, even hiring consultants to do this type of work requires some extra caution. Because of the kinds of things talked about, it should be conducted by senior practitioners who are confident, seasoned, experienced, and perhaps a bit long in the tooth. The consultants must be well endowed with the gravitas required to operate effectively at the executive level of an organization. Their overall demeanor must reek of experience, knowledge, and trustworthiness.

In summary, the Management Mirror is a high-risk—high-gain way of saying to the organization's top management: *Here is what you are doing and how you and your actions are perceived. Here is what your people and others in the organization are doing as a result of your actions. Here is how your individual and collective behavior as the top management team impact on day-to-day organizational performance and achievement of results. What are the team and its members going to do about it?* When your organizational intervention is systemic and cross-functional, having a senior team that is beginning to think systemically and cross-functionally about the nature of executive leadership is a distinctive plus, both for your project and for the whole organization moving forward.

Tools like the Management Mirror, employee satisfaction surveys, and 360° feedback surveys are generally discussed in terms of getting management to come to grips with their part in sustaining the "as is" situation. However, it must be pointed out that of even more importance to the issue of sustainability is the ability of the management group to understand its role in monitoring and maintaining the desired change.

A sustainable solution must always incorporate the specific roles and focus of management in maintaining and managing the new methods of working going forward, all focused on adding internal and external value.

When preparing to institute a significant organizational change, the management group of the organization would be well advised to keep in mind the words of one of our great American cartoonists, Walt Kelly, when his character Pogo stated to his cartoon colleagues, "We have met the enemy, and it is us!"

And equally, when designing a significant change in an organization, it behooves the designer to keep in mind the basic concept that solutions must include the ability of the management system to knowledgeably maintain and manage the solution going forward.

One of the most powerful ways to build in this ability of the management system to maintain and manage the solution going forward is to design the solution such that it is this same management group that is instrumental in rolling out and implementing the change.

I have heard many "experts" in Change Management make a strong point of the necessity of getting management support and sponsorship and of the importance of cascading the change from the top of the organization on down—which in most instances is indeed one of the best ways to proceed. It is interesting to me that while I hear this often, I rarely hear from these same people the corollary to this approach that I and a good many of my colleagues have learned—the lower the change efforts go into the organization, the less visible the "change consultants" must be to achieve sustainable success. The bottom line on achieving sustained results runs full circle back to the first chapter of this book on System. Sustainability of results rest primarily on how well integrated and aligned the solution is with the overall System. And by overall System I mean the System that will be there for the long haul—which by definition *does not* include the extraordinary people (often internal and/or external consultants) and efforts and systems that are unique to the change effort itself.

As has been mentioned previously, organizational culture (the accepted and valued behavioral/social patterns that exist among the people who make up the organization) is not an identifiable subsystem, it is rather a manifestation of the overall system. Long-term sustainability of any change is reflected in how well the "change" is embedded and embodied in the organizational culture.

Given the nature of continuous change today, potentially one of the most powerful aspects of sustained competitive edge today is an organizational culture that places a high value on innovation and change that is equal to the high value it places on desired results.

An organization that highly values results but equally values change and innovation will be one that seeks out continuous improvement. An organization of this type would view change and innovation as invigorating and central to maintaining excellent results.

It is a fair statement that true sustainability of high levels of performance will, in most cases today, include a requirement to build in the values of continual improvement as part and parcel of the overall organizational value system. All of the interest and focus in many circles on developing learning organizations is in reality just another way of labeling Continuous Improvement. An organization that incorporates adaptability and results-focused change as part of its central value system is an organization that is best suited for long-term positive results in this age of rapid and continuing evolution.

To a great extent, effectiveness as a senior executive is more about managing how you are perceived than it is about specific actions or demands. This self-awareness of perception and management of perception is central to effective executive management. Management, and especially executive management, is as much a performing art as it is a technology, it is as much about theater as it is about specifically requested or required actions.

My behavioral colleagues are far more right than wrong when they say behavior is all about rewards and incentives. Particularly when you incorporate perceived or anticipated rewards or recognition along with perceived or anticipated punishment (which includes being ignored or avoided).

Acting in accordance with perceived "real" desires or expectations of "the powers that be" is a primary driver for behavior and resulting performance in most organizations—for better or worse. It is much safer when the objectives are based on hard performance data based on a needs (not a wants) assessment.

Endnotes

1. Sustainability is often used in terms of "not making things worse... stop the damage." Kaufman (personal communication, April, 2008) has suggested an additional variable, "sustainability plus," where not only is damage stopped but also the entire System is returned to where it should be before human damage started its insidious work.

2. An evaluation framework and tools responsive to this is provided by Guerra-Lopez in another book in this series.

3. Quality is defined here as "fitness for us" as judged by internal and external stakeholders.

4. As pointed out in this book and extensively in the first book of this series (Kaufman, 2006) "needs" as used here are really "wants."

5. In this series, there is reference to three levels of planning and related results: Mega/Outcomes (societal), Macro/Outputs (organizational) and Micro/Products (individual). See Kaufman, 2006 for an extensive definition and justification. At this point, it is important that there are several required levels of planning, results, and consequences.

6. Also see Guerra-Lopez (2007) in this series for related guidance on useful evaluation and continual improvement.

Chapter 7
Monday Morning

Now that you have read this book, and hopefully the others in this series, it is time to take action. If you do not currently operate the way the books suggest but agree that it is the way you *should* operate, what do you do next? Where do you begin? The easy bit is deciding that you are going to approach the next project that you are given in a systemic way and "do it right." While that is a good resolution, it also side-steps the *real* issue in most organizations—which is, "How do we bring the entire organization into alignment—an alignment that adds measurable value internally and externally—over time and keep it there?" And of course, the more pointed question is "How do we proceed to get our function aligned with organizational intent and then maximize how we add value in aiding overall organizational effectiveness."

There are a number of things that can be done to start the movement toward where you can provide the most value to the organization.

A most critical, and hopefully obvious, first step as an individual is to make sure you can discuss the main issues impacting the organization in the same terms and words as the senior management of your organization. You have to "talk the talk" in a way that gives the perception that you can also "walk the walk" with the best of the management group. "Join" the management group by demonstrating you understand their issues and opportunities—which means being able to talk about the issues and opportunities intelligently in the terms your managers use.

If you are not sure how to start building this vocal capability, a simple start point is to first ascertain those among the management group that are generally considered to be "good about business." Find out what journals and business press they read or scan routinely and do the same.

Encourage those around you to do the same thing and try to make sure your meetings reflect the same broad issue and concerns that management is discussing—albeit in regard to how your function can support the organization in its endeavors.

This type of rigor can help significantly in keeping those around you thinking about the organization and external stakeholders in a systemic manner rather than becoming another "silo" function in the organization. And of course, work to align your own functional area with the overall organizational purpose as well as with Mega— external client and societal value added. The Alignment activities discussed in Chapter 2 can and should be applied to your own functional area.

However, possibly even before moving toward formal Alignment activities in your own function, there is some background and foundational work that should be done first. Work that will enable your function to more easily begin providing increased value to the organization.

Following are some basic things that can be recommended that will help in the movement of the overall HR function into better utilization of Human Performance Technology. One of the first is to get the function focused on the business approach and how HR can aid and abet the organizational intent, and core to this is thinking and acting systemically. The other critical variable is to make sure the business approach (or business case) also adds value to external clients and society.

If all the following things are in place, they will help enable the HR function to knowledgeably and effectively run projects in organizational effectiveness and also aid in the ability of the function to be proactive in increasing organizational results.

The starting point of being systemic is ensuring proper basic information and communication flows from across the organization into and out of your function.

Basic Information/Communication

Value Chain. Managing Organizational Effectiveness requires a high level value chain or process map for the organization that shows the flow of work through the organization. In other words, managing organizational effectiveness requires first and foremost a clear and documented understanding of how the goods and/or services provided by your organization are produced and delivered. This is a dynamic picture of how the organization works, from how raw materials and requests enter the organizational system to how they flow through it, and all the way through to delivery to the customer. Key elements of a value chain include the following:

- Identify the essential units and functions in the value chain

- Document where and how value is added by the organization

- Identify where and how critical elements of competitive edge or brand are created/maintained

- Identify where and how you will add measurable value to external clients and society

- Identify area by area whether results are team or individually based

- Identify and document cross-functional interdependencies for results

This value chain is one of the more critical systemic elements for proactive organizational management. Knowing where value is added and where critical elements are created informs where metrics, or some form of tracking, would be helpful. Areas where results are team based are obvious points to apply team-building and team-effectiveness processes. Cross-functional interdependencies are areas often overlooked in organizational management, particularly given the bias in most organizations to fix clear responsibility, or as many companies say, "We want one throat to choke."

As has been mentioned earlier in this book, team building is both a critical element of effective organizations and also, on its own, anti-systemic with the predictable property of reinforcing silo mentality. The counter to this anti-systemic element of team building is to couple team processes with partnering processes (team work between teams).

Business Plans. The importance of knowing where the executive group is attempting to take the organization and how the group determines how it is doing cannot be over stressed.

Balanced scorecards, key performance indicators (KPIs), and similar systems are quite helpful when available. If not available, they are well worth developing. Also of high value is the two-level business case proposed by Bernardez to include not only conventional business results, but societal results as well (Bernardez, 2005, 2008).

But regardless of what is available and what is not, the starting point is to ensure you are getting at least the same information about intent and how it is going as the executive group is getting. This is a critical step in making sense of what the organization is doing and where and why it is headed there.

Be it formal or informal, objective or intuitive, top down or bottom up, inclusive or exclusive, broad based or narrow, decisions are being made and direction is being provided to the organization. Understanding what, where, and how this is being done is another of the central keys to managing organizational performance.

Function and Unit Data. In many organizations, individual units and functions will quite normally develop their own internal measures of processes and results. Finding out what these are and getting on the distribution lists for this information are good ways to pull more information out of the organization with little additional effort.

Cross-Functional Processes and Dependencies. It is a curious thing to me that so many managers and executives will acknowledge that organizations are a System and that the various units must work well together to achieve maximum results and still do nothing about monitoring and actively managing these interdependencies.

A central property to any System is the effectiveness and efficiency of the interface between parts of the System. Almost by definition, the care and maintenance of these interfaces fall into the realm of whatever function takes on Human Performance Technology.

Interfaces require occasional facilitation in the management process. People who are "part" of the interface, or are identified with one side of the interface or the other, are by definition not viable facilitators of the interface when there are problems. This is a proper and necessary domain for the HPT practitioner.

Organizational System Data within HR. There are three categories of System data that fall within the normal jurisdiction of HR groups: intake data, exit data, and formal review data.

- Intake data track new employees into the organizational System. In the first 30 days, what is the match between the job the new employee expected and the reality? In the first 60 days, how is the job settling in, how is the management/supervisory relationship and team relationship (if appropriate) working out? And at 90 days, how "attuned" or not is the new employee to the focus and direction of the overall organization?

- Exit data—or systematic gathering and documenting of the views, opinions, comments, and suggestions from employees as they leave the organization, or even more valuably, 30 to 60 days after they have left the organiza- tion and are in new jobs—can provide very valuable views into the working of the organization.

- Formal review data are all too rarely analyzed and sum- marized in a systemic and systematic manner. Perform- ance reviews, goal/objective setting and accomplish- ment, grievances, warnings, coaching/counseling ses- sions, post training reviews, and other usually HR-based systems can also provide valuable data on the workings of the organization. This is particularly true when there is a process for systematic and systemic review, analysis, and summarization.

Organizational Culture and Sub-Culture Analysis. Remem- ber that culture is critical. As the late Geary Rummler noted, "If you put a great worker against a bad organization, the bad organization wins every time."

Where social patterns exist that do not aid the achievement of results, or may even impede desired results, you have targets of opportunity for increasing overall organizational effectiveness.

Development and Tracking of Management Values and Practices. A key part of the recommended alignment activities covered in this book centers on making the desired values and practices of management and supervision specific and measurable.

The expected values and practices should be made explicit and distributed to the total employee population as statements what they have a right to expect from their supervisors and managers.

Alignment of Your Own Function

Once you have verified that you know what the organization intends, and you have "plugged" yourself and your function into the organizational system by accessing as many of the above sources as possible, it is critical to align your HPT function with the organizational system within which you operate.

Even if the overall organization is not in a state of alignment, the HR or HPT functions must be aligned. The alignment model discussed in Chapter 2 is very scalable, and the same principles can be applied to aligning any group with internal and external demands and requirements.

Basic Tools and Processes to Systemically Work HPT Organizational Issues

Glossary of Business and Management Terms. It may seem a simplistic piece of busy work at first glance, but the development and maintenance of an organizational glossary covering common terms can be invaluable. In the training arena alone, particularly management and supervisory training, it is quite common to utilize programs and packages from various vendors for common generic topics.

Taken individually, each of these selections of packaged programs may make good sense, but all too often, this approach ends up adding some degree of confusion as to what is appropriate and accepted behavior due to varying definitions of terms and processes across various package vendors. The effort involved in aligning definitions will increase the uniform application of concepts and increase confidence in the understanding of what activities and results are desired. A common language of management and the business will also facilitate meetings and general communications across the organization. Common understanding is at the core of aligned activities and results.

360° Data. As mentioned above, once values and practices have been developed and agreed-upon 360° surveys can become powerful tools for managing and focusing management and supervisory behavior. A minimum of a yearly formal review of all agreed-upon management practices is a good general health check, providing not only individual management data, but also group and functional data and overall organizational patterns.

As more and more companies have more and more of their staff equipped with online access, a newer tool to support management actions is becoming available. The ability of an individual manager to send out short, focused surveys at his or her discretion on critical behaviors is a strong tool supporting individual manager remediation and development activities.

Training and Development Feedback. What is potentially one of the most timely and sensitive sources of operational information for HR groups occurs in departments large enough to have routine training classes running through the year.

The company is bringing groups of employees together around work topics—and people put into groups will talk. This is a huge source of information from throughout the organization. Collect it and analyze it for trends and patterns.

Going further, it is quite easy to co-opt some time for short and focused discussions or surveys around relevant issues where data are required. Yet, for whatever reason, most HR groups leave this source of data untapped—not even bothering to have instructors do a quick summary of what was discussed during the program for later review and analysis.

Basic Group Management Tools and Processes. There are a number of activities that do not occur often enough for any individual manager or supervisor to be expected to add them to his or her individual management skills. These are areas where the pro-active HR group can add value to overall organizational effectiveness.

- Fast start support:

  - New manager. A facilitated one-day New Manager Assimilation process can allow a team to cut out weeks and even months from the process of a group getting up to speed with a new manager. The productivity slow down common to transition periods can be significantly shortened.

  - New team. A facilitated one-to-two day New Team Formation process can significantly speed up the process of teams getting to know and getting comfortable with each other. As necessary, formal team-building activities can follow the formation process. Team building in new teams before the people have had a chance to "settle in" with each other is not a recommended activity. Give them a fast start first, and then if necessary do the formal team building.

- Group management/maintenance tools: In any organization, significant gains in managing for results and organizational effectiveness can be achieved by providing standardized but highly adaptable group management methodologies.

  - Team Building. Where groups of people must work in coordination to accomplish common goals and objectives. Team-building, team-assessment, and team-monitoring tools and processes are required to maximize effectiveness.

- Partnering. Where multiple groups of people have group inter-dependencies to accomplish all or parts of their tasks, standardized but adaptable processes to manage the cross-team relationships are important to overall organizational effectiveness.

- Tiger Teams/Action Learning. Basic toolkits and consulting/facilitation support for small, focused teams (often ad hoc teams) that will tackle process and infrastructure issues as they arise will significantly enhance the organization's ability to adapt to changing conditions and avoid stagnation.

- Meeting guides and norms. One of the most common complaints heard in organizations is in regard to the frequency, duration, and relative value of meetings that are part of daily organizational life—particularly for managers. A set of basic tools to aid and facilitate meetings can have significant impact as all meetings are not the same and should not be approached as if they were. Each of the following meetings have specific purposes and appropriate agendas and processes to maximize that purpose:

• Briefings
• Admin/operational meetings
• Decision-making meetings
• Alignment determinations
• Problem-solving meetings

  - Divergent processes
  - Convergent processes

Providing job aids, training, and facilitation as required to develop the conscious utilization of meetings in effective manners is a high payoff activity that will significantly aid organizational functioning.

- Goal/Objective/KPI Setting and Tracking System. Again, this is most valuable in environments where all managers and supervisors have online access.

Where the systems are in place, a relatively simple database tool for common documentation and tracking of targets across the organization is a highly valuable tool for monitoring and managing performance in a visible manner. It is also an empirical source of actionable data around organizational alignment.

- Performance Management tools. Tracking and analysis of patterns in things like performance appraisals and development plans across the company can also provide great insight into System-wide issues and opportunities.

- Networking Tools. Networking is critical to organizational effectiveness, especially as the size of the organization increases. Simply having tolls and processes to support networking sends a strong message to the organization of the importance of effective networking.

• Network documentation and analysis tools can be very helpful in aiding the development of proper and necessary networks across the organization. There are tools available that can guide people in developing, maintaining, and troubleshooting their networks. Facilitating networks is part of maintaining a System focus.

• Support and Challenge. The strongest aspect of organizational culture and values lies in the expectations and feedback that members of the organization provide to one another. The dual responsibility, particularly for managers and supervisors to both support others in their network *and* to challenge others to be even better is a powerful force for setting behavioral norms. Formalizing this activity by covering it in all management training and development activities and also putting it on the agenda at management meetings is highly recommended.

Communication Flows. In organizations large enough to have a communications department, there is a tendency to try to put overall responsibility for communications on this group. However, the reality is that this group's general expertise is in communication packaging and presentation, which also relates more to downward flow than upward flow.

It has always struck me as strange that while communication is almost always one of the identified problems, almost all actions around communication relate to downward flow. Yet, when I speak with CEOs and their immediate colleagues, I am struck by the fact that the smartest ones are forever lamenting their relative inability to get timely and accurate information from down in the organization as to what is working and what is not.

Robust process to encourage honest and timely upward flows of information about the functioning of the organization can be invaluable. Developing and maintaining these types of processes are not the domain of the standard communications group. They can and should be standard fare for the proactive HR group.

Leaving communications to the communications group leaves unanswered the actually greater question of facilitating useful communication flows, particularly flows in an upward direction with minimum distortion. This is about behavioral process management and also is usually a cross-functional issue, and as such is a very viable activity for an HPT-oriented group to take on.

- Upwards communications. Suggestion systems, hot lines, employee forums, town halls—all of these are reasonably common Systems to facilitate upward flow of thoughts, ideas, and issues. Their long-term viability will rest in how they are managed. They have to be safe, responsive (people know what is happening with their input), and easy to use—all of which relate to the human process more than the content. Design and implementation of human processes is precisely what HPT is about.

- Downwards communications. Here the purpose is generally briefing or informing. While the packaging and delivery methods may rest elsewhere in the organization, there is also quite often a requirement for people down the organization to react/respond to the downward communication—and once again we are into facilitating a human process. The HPT group should be deeply involved in these activities.

- Inwards communications. Rarely does the HR group have much involvement in customer input/reaction systems. However, the group should know what areas do have this type of information and get tapped into these information flows. Another potentially valuable inward information flow is what can be derived from vendors. If you can make your vendors comfortable enough with you to speak candidly about their impressions of your organization compared to other organizations they deal with, you can learn a lot about how the organization is viewed and the impression it makes externally.

The choices are yours. Either continue what is in place and only look for ways to work cheaper, faster, better, or rethink and reinvent the organizational culture to add measurable value within, as well as outside of, the organization.

Appendix A
Management Mirror

The Management Mirror is an activity for providing rich and deep feedback to executive teams on their individual and group impact on the organization for which they are responsible. Traditional 360° feedback and other such standard appraisals have a notably weak impact in the Executive suite. The generic broad brush of standardized surveys in general does not have sufficient "face validity" with most executives.

The Management Mirror is a qualitative-based research methodology to provide specific, very individualized feedback to executives in a manner that is difficult, if not impossible, to glaze over lightly. It is designed to be very poignant and very personal.

This type of data is the richest in terms of specific feedback and impact, but is also the most costly to gather and extremely easy to contaminate (unconsciously steer, direct or otherwise manipulate the data that are gathered) during the collection process.

Qualitative methodologies, when done well, are by their very nature quite individual and specific. The researcher who gathers the data, however, has to be a highly accomplished interviewer, well versed and experienced in the intense rigors of qualitative data gathering.

What follows are two sample reports. These reports are "sanitized" versions (names of the individuals and the company have been eliminated) of actual summary reports from a real situation.

The reports are referred to as Summary reports as they are, by design, not a complete and detailed review of all the findings. Part of the feedback process is to force the subject executive manager to take careful notes of his or her own during the feedback session. The feedback is delivered verbally by a senior consultant who personally conducted at least half of the interviews for this particular manager.

The executive manager knows that he or she is going to have to give a full briefing to his or her peers and boss in a management meeting in a few days. The consultant doing the briefing will also attend the briefing to fill in as necessary if the executive team member happens to forget anything.

The executive knows that he or she will only get a written summary of the findings, and it is up to the executive to make sure his or her notes have all the necessary detail they require to enable a thorough briefing to the executive's peers.

This particular tactic aids considerably in getting the executive to focus on listening carefully and fully understanding the feedback rather than defending against it, listening selectively, or otherwise "misunderstanding" what they are told.

A reference is made to a graphic piece of feedback: Leader as a Model profile. This refers to the Energy Investment Model. In this model, the subject manager is rated from 1 to 10 (1 being low and 10 being high) along two scales.

One scale is Energy. To what extent does this manager put personal energy and drive into making sure the business succeeds?

The second scale is Attitude. What type of attitude does this manager exhibit when dealing with the requirements of the business?

The person rating the manager is asked to make two marks on each scale: the manager's average position on both scales when things are going well, and the manager's average position on a bad day when things are not going well.

The two scales are graphically represented as two axes: Attitude is the vertical axis and Energy is the horizontal axis. The bottom left hand corner is 1 on both scales and the top right hand corner is 10 on both scales.

The four quadrants of the model can then be labeled with descriptive labels:

Low energy, negative attitude = Walking Dead
Low energy, positive attitude = Spectators
High energy, negative attitude = Well Poisoner
High energy, positive attitude = Player

This feedback focuses on what the manager is modeling in terms of Attitude and Energy in his or her daily behavior.

The graphic feedback sheet is presented as a scatter gram with each point on the scatter gram identified with the initials of the rater. This is an example of one of many used widely:

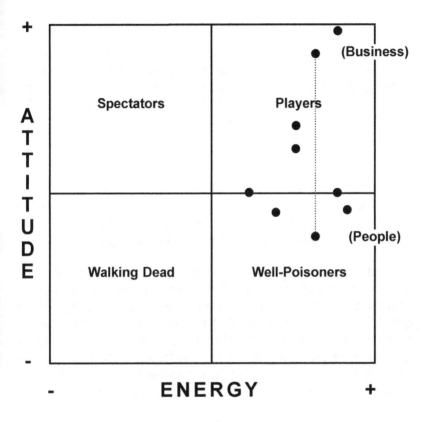

[DATE]

Dear [Managing Director:]

Attached is your individual feedback report, in conjunction with the senior team **Management Mirror** exercise that we have been conducting for your organization over the past few months. You will recall, in initiating this effort, you said, "We want to focus on how we get more out of the team effort as managers—not just us—all the 52 managers in the hierarchy...but it must start with us."

The purpose of the senior management analysis is, again in your words, "to take a look in the mirror as it were—so that we can begin to work more effectively as a team and set the pattern for the way we do business in (this organization)."

The **Management Mirror** process consisted of one-on-one interviews with all members of the senior team and of all direct reports to members of the senior team. Additionally, focus groups were conducted within the departments of each senior team member as appropriate. These interviews and focus groups were primarily focused on gathering perceptions about the senior team and its individual members based on behavior rather than verbiage (how you "walk"—not how you "talk").

The collective findings and implications of this analysis are the focus of the scheduled senior team meeting. Your attached individual feedback report—your personal "look in the mirror"—is presented in the following sections of this report:

> **General Summary**—a narrative description of you as a leader and manager, as perceived by your direct reports, and a sampling of staff at the level below your direct reports. Again, emphasis here is on your behavior—what you are seen as doing day-to-day, and

the messages your behavior sends and perceptions it creates.

Leader-as-Model Profile—where your direct reports place you on the Energy Investment Model (*Pleasers, Spectators, Walking Dead, Well Poisoners*).

Functional Leadership Data—how you are rated by your direct reports in performing the leadership functions of Direction, Motivation, and Guidance to your organization and how effectively you have communicated messages of quality, customer focus, and strategy to your organization.

We hope that you will find this feedback helpful as the leader of your organization—and that the collective team interaction enables the senior team to become more effective, to the benefit of the entire organization.

We stand ready to assist you in taking appropriate action based on this feedback in any way you think we may be helpful.

Sincerely,

Bob Carleton, Senior Partner
Claude Lineberry, Senior Partner

General Summary

There are two broad themes that come through in regard to what it is like to work for you. The first of these is characterized by the following types of phrases:

- High demand and constant pressure
- Very focused with clear goals
- Lots of energy and enthusiasm

When these phrases are combined with the comments made by most of your team about being given lots of latitude, and you're being supportive with advice and being willing to listen, it makes for a very positive picture. All of this adds up to the potential for a high-performing organization.

Unfortunately there is an equally strong darker side. This side is characterized by the following phrases:

- Ruthless, tough, lots of stick and little carrot
- Impatient and quick tempered
- Be careful about what and how you say things
- Never cross him

This set can make for a very cautious environment where people are more concerned about avoiding pain than pushing out the boundaries. This type of demeanor leads to a very inward and upward focus in an organization where business focus and intelligent customer focus can get lost.

When we go into what is required to be on your good side, this potentially split impact really comes through. While there is a clear thread of deliver results and meet your commitments, it has a tone of doing so because of consequences with you if staff don't, rather than because it's the right thing for the business. The tone of responding to you first and the business second is really underlined by the fact that six of your direct reports clearly state that keeping you happy means doing whatever you ask for and doing it damn quick.

You do have some stronger people who clearly have the message of speaking up and not being intimidated as a critical piece of what you expect of them. This minority talks about making a difference to the business, being innovative, and being honest with you. The group that says this, however, is clearly a minority who feels comfortable with you and your style.

There is a small group in the middle that is best characterized by the statement "*don't* just agree with him, unless his mind is made up when you don't dare rock the boat."

When asked to describe your strengths, the list was relatively short and succinct. Vision, energy, and clarity of thought were immediate responses from almost everyone. There were numerous references to your business acumen, your ability to not get bogged down, and your willingness to make tough decisions. There was general agreement that you have really advanced the business and are making things happen.

On the weaknesses side, people seemed inclined to be a bit more prolific with many references to a short temper and being very unforgiving for failure to win. High control "needs" and quickly expressed frustration/irritation were also referenced freely. Almost everyone seemed to have ready, personal stories of very off-putting interactions on more than one occasion. There seemed to be a general unease about interaction with you, primarily due to uncertainty about what you might take personally, resulting in a demeaning emotional outburst. All of this results in a tendency to "walk on eggshells" around you and be a bit cautious about timing and content. At minimum, there appears to be slightly more concern about reading you than the content of the interaction or the focus of the business.

The advice from your team continues to reflect the double theme. There is a good strong message about keeping it up and continuing on because you're clearly on the right path. They don't want you to waiver or begin to compromise.

The second message is about slowing down/easing up a little and spending a bit more time on building relationships and understanding your people better.

The slightly slower speed is to allow people to catch up and get on board. The building relationships is about easing some of the tension and fear, and hopefully improving some of the team's inner workings.

Priorities

When asked what your top three to five priorities are, your 13 direct reports generated a widely divergent list of 28 different items.

A total of 10 different items were given the number one position.

Ten different items were also in the number two spot, including 7 items completely different from the first 10.

The number three spot generated another 5 additional items.

This is a long way of saying that you effectively have no team agreement on priorities. If we just go to a simple frequency count, the top five would be as follows:

1.	Achieve synergy with the management team	5
2.	Deliver financial results	4
	Complete change agenda	4
	Motivate staff	4
5.	Quality	3
	Enhance customer confidence	3
	Be creative	3

It is interesting that while synergy of the management team was mentioned most (by 5 of the 13 people), no one ranked it as first or second priority.

Leader-as-Model Profile

Your direct reports placed you on the Energy Investment Model in the following manner:

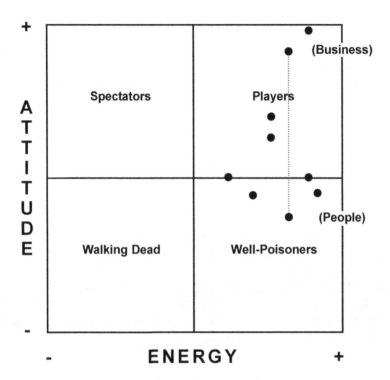

Skip Level Placement of Senior Team

    Total Number of Raters: 73
    Total Number of Data Points: 485
    Total Data Point Averages: 72.5% Player, 27.5% other
    Average of Averages: 72.8%, 27.2% others

Your Personal Score: 31 Total Data Points, 63.6% Player, 36.4% other

Functional Leadership Data

1. The goals and objectives communicated are helpful in establishing direction for daily activities.	Avg. = 7.55 Range = 5–9

With only two 5s and the rest mostly 8s and 9s, the overall rating is quite good.

The lower scores included comments about "the document" alone not being enough and conflict between long-term and short-term knee jerks.

2. The vision and mission described for the business and its future is helpful and exciting to staff.	Avg. = 7.18 Range = 5–10

Most of the scores here were 7s and 8s with the lower end anchored with two 5s and a 6.

The marginally lower rating here compared to the above item relates to the vision not getting down into the organization.

The single 10 came from the one person with the least staff. If the 10 was backed out, the overall rating would be a 6.9—clearly into the problematic range.

3. Reward and recognition are used in a way that encourages people to do the right things.	Avg. = 7.18 Range = 4–9

You have one person who is personally very unhappy, and two people who feel the rewards systems aren't good, particularly further down in the organization.

Everyone else feels this is an okay area with scores of 7 to 9.

There were a few comments about more stick than carrot in your general style.

4. Confidence is expressed in the staff's ability to get things right and succeed in the future.	Avg. = 7.01 Range = 5–9

The focus of the concern here was in regard to people outside of the senior team. A number of comments were made about the MG (management grade) grades being in limbo.

If the lone 9 is removed, the overall score drops into the 6s and again clearly indicates a problem.

5. Assistance in the form of advice, coaching, and counseling is provided to help staff do a better job.	Avg. = 6.64 Range = 4–8

The commentary here was pretty consistent that you do not have a coaching style. The general view was that it doesn't come naturally to you.

6. If everyone modeled their behavior on that of the managing director, this would be a more effective operation.	Avg. = 7.27 Range = 2–9

If the lone 2 is dropped off, the average jumps to a 7.80, which says that in general your team feels you are a good model.

The only hesitations were around

- the problem in item 5 above, and
- the concern about not taking people with you, which relates to item 2 above.

[DATE]

Dear [Executive Team Member]:

Attached is your individual feedback report summary in conjunction with the senior team exercise that we have been conducting over the past few months. You will recall, in initiating this effort, that it was said, "we *need*[1] to focus on how we get more out of the team effort as managers—not just us—all members of the hierarchy... but it must start with us."

The purpose of the senior management analysis is "to take a look in the mirror as it were so that we can begin to work more effectively as a team and set the pattern for the way we do business in our organization."

The **Management Mirror** process consisted of one-on-one interviews with all members of the senior team, and of all direct reports to members of the senior team. Additionally, focus groups were conducted within the departments of each senior team member as appropriate. These interviews and focus groups were primarily focused on gathering perceptions about the senior team and its individual members based on behavior rather than verbiage (how you "walk"—not how you "talk").

The collective findings and implications of this analysis are the focus of the senior team meeting scheduled for the near future. Your attached individual feedback report summary—your personal "look in the mirror" is presented in the following sections of this report:

General Summary—a narrative description of you as a leader and manager, as perceived by your boss, your peer managers/team members, your direct reports, and a sampling of staff at the level below your direct reports. Again, emphasis here is on your behavior— what you are seen as doing day-to-day, and the messages your behavior sends and perceptions it creates.

Leader-as-Model Profile—where your boss and peers place you on the Energy Investment Model (*Pleasers, Spectators, Walking Dead, Well Poisoners*) and where your direct reports place you. A brief narrative interpretation is provided on both placements.

Functional Leadership Data—how you are rated by your direct reports in performing the leadership functions of Direction, Motivation, and Guidance to your organization and how effectively you have communicated messages of quality, customer focus, and strategy to your organization.

We hope that you will find this feedback helpful as a key leader of your organization and that the collective team interaction enables the senior team to become more effective to the benefit of the entire organization.

We stand ready to assist you in taking appropriate action based on this feedback in any way you think we may be helpful.

Sincerely,

Bob Carleton, Senior Partner
Claude Lineberry, Senior Partner

General Summary

Your People

Interestingly, most of the 10 direct reports interviewed expressed a strong view that they want you to succeed and be part of that success and that you have the potential to succeed. But they also indicated that you are not letting them help you as fully as possible through elements of your style that frustrate, block, limit, demoralize, and/or anger them.

Their frustration at this perceived paradox is heightened by an overall favorable view of you as a business man and human being. You truly are, in their eyes, your own worst enemy.

In describing what it's like to work for you—what kind of boss you are—they discriminate based on your mercurial nature into good day/bad day characteristics.

The former good day list includes energy, passion, vision, strength, excitement, focus, kindness, and concern for the individual.

The latter bad day list finds you impatient, rude, brusque, unpredictable, moody, callous, inconsistent, and with an almost total disregard for the individual.

This dichotomy is exacerbated by the unpredictable swing from good to bad—sometimes over minutes rather than days.

While the tougher, more resilient of your direct reports have figured out how to cope with your schizophrenic management style, others have not.

All see your potential value to the organization and, in fact, profile your strengths in descriptors that closely match the positive attributes and strengths of the managing director. Discrimination between you is largely in the nature of your identified weaknesses.

Those strengths include energy and quickness, clear vision, financial focus, courage, total dedication to the business, openness and contention, and a heart of gold.

The weaknesses that limit those strengths are mostly in behavioral style rather than competence.

You are found to be abrasive to the point of cruelty, inconsiderate, a poor listener, impulsive, one who manages selectively ("beats up on the weak and timid, respects those who push back"), and a poor manager of your time. The perceived net result is that your very significant value to your division is being limited or denied to the organization by elements of your management style—elements that seem trivial but are highly visible as compared to the strengths, and this compromises the value you add to the organization.

All feel that the situation is potentially damaging to the effectiveness of the multi-team structure of the new organization and that remediation of the situation is overdue.

Your direct reports and your peers know that you ask for and value feedback. They say you attempt to act on it and succeed for a short time, but then seem to always fall back into the good day/bad day pattern.

Priorities

When asked to infer your priorities from your behavior and action there was little hesitation. Your direct reports listed, in rank order:

1st Priority:
Success of the reorganization

2nd Priority:
Build effective teams—management, hub, and shift

3rd Priority:
Establish effective multidirectional communication within your geographic area

4th Priority:
Ensure customer retention through customer satisfaction

5th Priority:
Achieve individual and team compliance to processes, practices, and standards

The animal that your behavior suggests to your direct reports represented a menagerie of the following:

- Definitely not a bunny
- Rhino (strong, thick skin, shortsighted, nervous, provokable)
- Vicious dog (might lie quietly, might attack)
- Cape Buffalo (aggressive, can show compassion by backing off from kill)
- Lion (loud roar, unpredictably aggressive)
- Elephant (capable of wreaking havoc without knowing it, intelligent, family oriented, kind)

Key Messages

In terms of key messages that you have communicated about strategy, quality, and the customer, the message about strategy is the strongest. The reorganization and strategy is seen as directly linked and aligned with overall corporate strategy.

There is confusion around quality, ranging from it meaning customer satisfaction through service delivery and recovery, to—at the junior A-scale level—a belief that "quality has been called off, it's just production now."

The customer is defined as all external customers, of various priority, and all cargo warehouses and departments.

Advice that your direct reports hope you will heed includes the following:

- Get control of the negative elements of your management style and minimize/eliminate them.
- Begin building visibility on the cargo warehouse floor ("Look, for goodness sake, get down on the floor and meet your people!").
- Listen (and look like you're listening).
- Organize and delegate to get more time, and then manage that time effectively to personally get it right the first time (avoiding a "ready – fire – aim" tendency).

- Above all, treat people as human beings in all your dealings with them.

Asked how to stay on your good side, direct reports listed behaviors that include standing up to you, letting you know the news—good and bad—in a timely manner, being willing to give time and effort required, being positive and energetic, and playing to your mood.

Your Peers

An overall positive view of you is held by your colleagues on the senior management team, as reflected in their placement of you on the Energy Investment Model (enclosed). They like your honesty, energy, and commitment. You are found to be results oriented, business focused, and financially adept. The difficulty of your task is recognized, and the perceptions to date are that you are doing the right things.

There is concern with your high control requirements, stubbornness on positions, relationship with your peers, and your willingness/ability to listen. The main concern is with the negative aspects of your style and its impact on your people, and on the multiteam structure that is key to the success of the reorganization.

Your peers are supportive of you, and see your success as key to their success, short term and longer term. The concern is that you will not realize the best out of your people and therefore prevent yourself from succeeding.

Leader-as-Model Profile

Your direct reports placed you on the Energy Investment Model in the following manner:

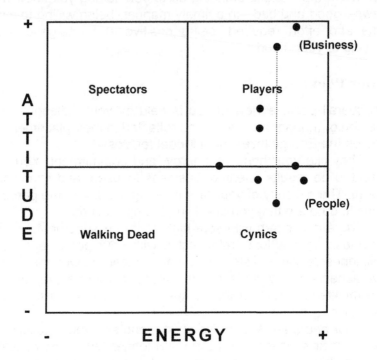

Skip Level Placement of Senior Team

> Total Number of Raters: 73
> Total Number of Data Points: 485
> Total Data Point Averages: 72.5% Player, 27.5% other
> Average of Averages: 72.8%, 27.2% others

Your Personal Score: 31 Total Data Points, 63.6% Player, 36.4% other

Functional Leadership Data

1. **The goals and objectives communicated are helpful in establishing direction for daily activities.**
This has more to do with personal rather than written direction, focusing on behaviors in meetings and interpersonal contact. Very wide range of scores.

   Average = 5.84
   Range = 3–9

2. **The vision described for the business and its future is helpful and exciting to staff.**
Your highest score, having to do with articulation of the "big" picture and your ownership and passion for it. Again, wide range of scores.

   Average = 6.20
   Range = 3–7

3. **Reward and recognition are used in a way that encourages people to do the right things.**
This represents your good day score—as one respondent gave you a 7 – 3 good day/bad day rating.

   Average – 4.91
   Range = 3–7

4. **Confidence is expressed in staff's ability to get things right and succeed in the future.**
Discussion indicates that this varies depending on whether you inherited the individual staff member or appointed the said member.

   Average = 5.61
   Range = 1–8

5. **Assistance in the form of advice, coaching, and counseling is provided to help staff do a better job.**
A huge range of scores over 10 respondents, pointing to selective management.

   Average = 5.61
   Range = 1–8

6. **If everyone modeled their behavior on that of the manager, this would be a more effective operation.**
*A profile of your strengths would rate much higher. This score is a comment on the impact of the negative elements of your style.

   Average = *3.53
   Range = 1–6

Endnote

1. Note that the use of "need" in this case is only because it is a direct quote from existing materials. This is in distinction to the use of "need" in this book and series as a noun: a gap in results, not a gap in processes or resources.

Appendix B
Organizational Culture
Assessing Organizational Culture
Off-the-Shelf or Customized Cultural Assessment?

Organizations that wish to assess and profile their culture and perhaps the culture of a target company in conjunction with cultural due diligence are faced with a choice between "off-the-shelf" assessment models and "customized" assessment models. While there has been significant advancement in the understanding of organizational culture over the past 10 years, the overall field is still in its infancy. As of today, there is no single unified theory or assessment model of organizational culture that can anticipate and account for all the potential variables of any given organizational culture.

There are currently at least 25 off-the-shelf attributional models of organizational culture in existence—models fundamentally based on *quantitative measurement* of *assumed cultural factors* or attributes. Most popular among them are the *Denison Organizational Culture Survey*, the *Organizational Culture Inventory (OCI)* and the *Hagberg Culture Assessment Tool*. The developers of these models and many others have been able to validate at least some aspects of their modes. This simply means that they have been able to demonstrate statistically that the variables (attributes), or at least some of the variables that they portend to measure, can indeed be measured reliably. All have the appearance of science and dramatic graphic displays.

These attributional models begin with quantitative measurement of assumed cultural factors, provide no color or granularity of local cultural variations, require subsequent *qualitative* research for effective cultural integration, and introduce the confusion of a new non-business vocabulary to the organization. They are predicated on the assumption that one size fits all. It doesn't.

The immediate problem that should be glaring to any researcher is that there are indeed multiple attributional models, each containing some of these assumed variables, with no reliable commonality between them. This means there are multiple models of equal potential validity. How do you choose which one to use in any given organizational situation? Each model was developed from intense study of a few companies, but to arbitrarily choose any one of them for use in any given company is to commit a classic Type II Research Error—*to assume that the attributes of one group apply to another different group when it has already been shown that there are different groups with different variables at play.*

If there was one unified theory or comprehensive listing of validated attributes across all cultural studies, this would not be the case. But given the variety of validated models with different measurable attributes, reasonably extensive *qualitative* research (interviews and focus groups possibly leading to customized surveys) is required to ascertain which attributes apply to a particular company at a particular time in order to make an accurate choice and avoid the Type II error.

Second, the current inventory of attributional models measures at a very high level of abstraction from the daily grind of on-the-job behaviors. This means that even if the right model is chosen for the company in question that did measure the relevant variables, it is still necessary to interpret how these variables relate to the daily work behaviors. The only way to get this data accurately is to engage in collection of *qualitative* data—detailed interviews, focus groups, and observations—to determine what the daily behaviors are that tie into the measured attributes.

Third, none of the current models are able to distinguish between *value-laden differences* and *non-value-laden differences*. A brief example of the problem: Two companies are merging. One has a culture that involves extensive use of e-mail, and the other does not use e-mail. In this instance, it is simply an issue of technology availability, and there is no inherent value system underlying the difference. In this case, the integration of the two cultures around this difference could well be limited to provision of the missing e-mail technology and a simple training program on the use of e-mail.

But now consider two other companies with the same difference in e-mail usage that are about to merge. One company has made a conscious decision to severely limit e-mail usage as the staff feel that professionals talk to each other rather than send e-mails to a person down the corridor, which they feel is impersonal and rude. The other company has made a conscious decision to heavily utilize e-mail as the staff feel true professionals do not interrupt one another by simply "dropping by" another's office. Courtesy is to send an e-mail that the other professional can access when ready and dropping in would be perceived as rude and unprofessional. Now you have a *value-laden difference,* and the merging of these two cultures is an entirely different matter—and one in which simple training would probably exacerbate the problems and in no way be a part of the resolution.

This one would require careful integration, planning groups, and careful change management, with particular attention paid to emotions and preconceived ideas. We know of no attributional model that will uncover this distinction. Distinguishing between value-laden and non-value-laden differences requires in-depth interviews and focus groups to ascertain the nature and depth of the feelings—or intensive qualitative research.

Fourth is the issue of granularity—or breadth and depth of variables—detailed enough to distinguish between units and divisions in the organizational cultures being studied. This level of granularity is critical to a responsive and prescriptive integration plan. Different parts of any given company or companies will have their own subtle and not so subtle differences in the application or adherence to the greater overall culture(s) variables. Sufficient granularity to enable an effective integration plan for each area of the company or companies involved requires some degree of interviews and/or focus groups and/or targeted surveys designed to measure the particular variables at play in that particular situation.

Finally, all of the above problems are issues in trying to align the culture variables of any one company. In a merger, the problems are multiplied by the number of companies merging as each will have potentially unrelated attributes critical to them that may be irrelevant in the others—which means even selecting a single correct attributional model is impossible. In summary, surveys based on attributional models do not provide sufficient local color to make the connections between the measured attributes and daily behavior clear and understandable; do not even attempt to measure all the variables that may be in play; provide no distinctions between value-laden differences and non-value-laden differences; and do not provide sufficient local granularity to allow for informed adjustment for local unit or division uniqueness. Qualitative research is required to ascertain which survey instruments available are appropriate for any given company. Qualitative research is also required to provide the necessary detail of how the measured attributes relate to daily behavior.

A simpler and more efficient approach is to use a customized culture assessment model utilizing a *qualitative research design* based on a *functional model of culture* and get all data required in one research activity. A functional model does not pretend to describe or assume the cultural attributes at play. Instead it defines the areas of daily organizational life in which cultural differences play out and gathers in-depth qualitative data in these areas that will, in one process, ascertain the variables that exist in any given company or companies that are value-laden and how they play out in daily behavior.

This will then enable the cultural research effort, if desired, to design a quantitative survey that can be sent out to the total organizational population to get further detail on the depth and breadth of the critical variables, area by area throughout the companies being researched. This in turn can provide the detail necessary to plan and implement an informed integration plan.

An example: Recently a client was considering an off-the-shelf culture survey. The survey under consideration measures 12 assumed cultural attributes with 120 survey items. It also provides an additional 39 supplemental questions for the user. No qualitative data are collected or reported.

Is something this simplistic going to provide the detail necessary to uncover the subtleties and nuances of operating differences in daily behavior across a global company of 125,000 employees in 22 countries, with at least four separate and distinct company cultures/subcultures that we know of that are alive and well.

We would contend, and the client agreed, that the answer is "no" and that it is not a rational assumption to think otherwise. An in-depth qualitative research design, however, does not have these limitations. A well-designed series of interviews and focus groups, however, will yield a wealth of qualitative data that are rich and robust and of much more utility and value than the results of any "off-the-shelf" quantitative survey.

The functional model of organizational culture provides the basic background for a customized culture assessment.

Twelve Domains of Organizational Culture
A Functional Model

The organizational culture (the social patterns and belief systems) of an organization can be ascertained from how people respond to open-ended questions covering each of the following 12 topic areas.

1. **Intended direction and results.** What is the business plan about? What is the intent and purpose of the organization and what results are expected from the activities? Does it include all levels, including external clients and society? Most specifically, how are all of these things talked about, described, and communicated at each level in the organization?

2. **Key measures.** What does the company measure and why? How available are these measures across the company? What are the formal and informal rewards, recognitions, punishments, and consequences associated with each of these measures? Are they used?

3. **Key business drivers.** What are the primary issues, opportunities, and threats that are driving the business plan? What particular thing or things does the organization seem to be focused on? What are considered to be the primary differentiators of this company from the rest of the competition? How is the industry and competition defined? Is the focus on market share, margin, volume, niche, prestige, societal value added?

4. **Infrastructure.** How is the company organized and what are the nature of the reporting relationships? How do units and functions relate to each other and access each other? What policies and procedures are in place? What systems are in place that are primarily designed to restrict and control activities? What systems are in place that are primarily designed to enable, guide, and support activities in the

organization? How do people talk about and describe the infrastructure elements of the organization?

5. **Organizational practices.** What formal information and tracking systems are in place in the organization? How much flexibility is allowed at each level and function in the organization? How intrusive or invasive are organizational policies and procedures into daily operations? How is policy and procedure disseminated and enforced—if at all? Are there incentives for value-added performance?

6. **Leadership and management practices.** What is the balance of transactional versus transformational behaviors in management at each level of the organization? What value or belief systems are in place at each level in the organization regarding employees, customers, shareholders, decision making, costs, quality, value added, and how does it show in employee vocabulary and behavior? How does business intention get implemented through the management system?

7. **Supervisory practices.** What dynamics are at play in the immediate oversight/ support of those doing the work? What is the nature of the interactions between supervisors and employees? How do supervisors spend their time? What is the balance between employee focus and product/service delivery focus?

8. **Work practices.** How is the actual work performed? Is it an individual or team focus? What degree of control (if any) does the worker or team have on work flow, quality, rate, tools, supplies?

9. **Technology use.** How does the organization view technology internally? How is technology used internally and externally by customers, vendors, suppliers, and other agents and agencies? How current is the organization's technology? What are people accustomed to in technological resources and support?

**10. Physical environment—how does the workplace look
and feel?** Are there open work spaces or private spaces
and how is it determined? Is the work area one of high
security or open access? What are the buildings, ground,
and furniture like? How much personalization of individual
or team workspace is allowed, if any?

11. Perception and expectations. What do employees think is
important at each level in the organization? How aligned
are the expectations and perceptions of each function and
level with other functions and levels in the organization?
What is the perceived level and nature of "support and
challenge" across the organization?

12. Cultural indicators and artifacts. How do people speak to
and address each other? How do people dress and what is
the match between formal and informal work hours? What
sorts of activities, if any, does the company sponsor and
what are they like?

Some of you may have noticed that there is nothing in the
list about Myths, Legends, and Heroes. These are things that
many of the writers on organizational culture, or societal culture
for that matter, point out as key indicators of beliefs and cultural
values. These issues are most pointedly not being ignored. If
you inquire into the above 12 domains and ask for stories and
examples in each area, the Myths, Legends, and Heroes of the
organization, to the extent that there are any, will come out in
clear detail.

Now, one last closing word on ascertaining organizational
values and beliefs and organizational culture: the short and
simple direct approach of asking staff about these topics
directly will rarely work and is not advised.

About this Series

This is the fifth of six books to define and deliver measurable Performance Improvement. Each volume defines a unique part of a fabric: a fabric to define, develop, implement, and continually improve human and organizational performance success. In addition, the series relates to the professional standards in the field.[1]

Why This Series?

Human and Organizational Performance Accomplishment—some call the field HPT (Human Performance Technology)—is of great interest to practitioners and clients alike who intend to deliver successful results and payoffs that are based on research, ethics, and solid concepts and tools. The author of each book provides a practical focus on a unique area, and each book is based on 10 principles of professional contribution.

Each book "stands alone" as well as knits with all the others. Together they:

1. Define the field of HPT and Performance Improvement based on the principles of ethical and competent practice.

2. Provide specific guidance on six major areas of professional practice.

3. Are based on a common framework for individual and organizational performance accomplishment.

4. Reinforce the principles that drive competent and ethical Performance Improvement.

There is a demand for an integrated approach to Human and Organizational Performance Accomplishment/Human Performance Technology. Many excellent books and articles are available (some by the proposed authors), but none covers the entire spectrum of the basic concepts and tools, nor do they give the integrated alignment or guidance that each of these six linked books provides.

This series is edited by Roger Kaufman (Ph.D., CPT), Dale Brethower (Ph.D.), and Richard Gerson (Ph.D., CPT). The six books and the authors are:

Book One: *Change, Choices, and Consequences: A Guide to Mega Thinking and Planning.* Roger Kaufman, Professor Emeritus, Florida State University, Roger Kaufman & Associates, and Distinguished Research Professor, Sonora Institute of Technology

Book Two: *Performance Analysis: Knowing What to Do and Why.* Dale Brethower, Professor Emeritus, Western Michigan University and Research Professor, Sonora Institute of Technology

Book Three: *Performance by Design.* Ryan Watkins, Associate Professor, George Washington University, Senior Research Associate, Roger Kaufman & Associates, and former NSF Fellow

Book Four: *Achieving High Performance.* Richard Gerson, Ph.D., CPT, Gerson Goodson, Inc.

Book Five: *Implementation and Management of Performance Improvement Plans.* Robert Carleton, Senior Partner, Vector Group

Book Six: *Evaluating Impact: Evaluation and Continual Improvement for Performance Improvement Practitioners.* Ingrid Guerra-López, Ph.D., Assistant Professor, Wayne State University and Associate Research Professor, Sonora Institute of Technology as well as Research Associate, Roger Kaufman & Associates

How This Series Relates to the Professional Performance Improvement Standards

The following table identifies how each book relates to the 10 Standards of Performance Technology[2] (identified by numbers in parentheses) pioneered by the International Society for Performance Improvement (ISPI).[3] In the table below, an "X" identifies coverage and linking, and a checkmark (✓) indicates major focus.

This series, by design, goes beyond these standards by linking everything an organization uses, does, produces, and delivers to adding measurable value to external clients and society. This six pack, then, builds on and then goes beyond the current useful criteria and standards in the profession and adds the next dimensions of practical, appropriate, as well as ethical tools, methods, and guidance of what is really required to add value to all of our clients as well as to our shared society.

	Focus on Results (1)	Take a System Approach (2)	Add Value (3)	Partner (4)	Needs Assessment (5)	Performance Analysis (6)	Design to Specification (7)	Selection, Design, & Development (8)	Implementation (9)	Evaluation & Continuous Improvement (10)
Book 1	✓	✓	X	✓	✓	X	X	X		✓
Book 2	X	✓	✓	X		✓	✓			X
Book 3	X	X	X			✓	✓	✓		X
Book 4	X	X	X	X		✓	X	✓	✓	X
Book 5	X	✓	✓	✓		✓	✓		✓	✓
Book 6	✓	✓	✓	X	✓				X	✓

All of this will only be useful to the extent to which this innovative practice becomes standard practice. We invite you to the adventure.

Roger Kaufman, Ph.D., CPT
Dale Brethower, Ph.D.
Richard Gerson, Ph.D., CPT

Endnotes

1. The Standards of Performance Technology developed by the International Society for Performance Improvement, Silver Spring, Maryland.

2. Slightly modified.

3. Another approach to standardization of performance are a set of competencies developed by the American Society for Training and Development (ASTD), *ASTD Models for Human Performance Improvement,* 1996, which are more related to on-the-job performance.

References

Bernardez, M. (2005). Achieving Business Success by Developing Clients and Community: Lessons from Leading Companies, Emerging Economies and a Nine Year Case Study. *Performance Improvement Quarterly, 18*(3). 37–55.

Bernardez, M. (2008). Minding the business of business: tools and models to design and measure wealth creation. Cd. Obregon, Mexico. The Performance Improvement Institute of The Sonora (Mexico) Institute of Technology.

Bernardez, M. (2005). Achieving Business Success by Developing Clients and Community: Lessons from Leading Companies, Emerging Economies and a Nine Year Case Study. *Performance Improvement Quarterly, 18*(3), 37–55.

Bernardez, M. (May–June, 2008). Sailing the Winds of "Creative Destruction": Educational Technology during economic downturns. *Educational Technology.*

Bertalanffy, L. Von. (1968). *General systems theory.* New York: George Braziller.

Brethower, D. M. & Dams, P-C. (1999:Jan.). Systems Thinking (and Systems Doing). *Performance Improvement, 38*(1), 37–52.

Buckley, W. (Ed.). (1968). *Modern systems research for the behavioral Scientist.* Chicago, IL: Aldine Publishing Company.

Davis, I. (2005, May 26). The Biggest Contract. *The Economist.* 375(8428), 87.

Drucker, P. F. (1973). *Management: Tasks, Responsibilities, Practices.* New York: Harper & Row.

Guerra-Lopez, I. (2007). Evaluating Impact: Evaluation and Continual Improvement for Performance Improvement Practitioners. Amherst, MA: HRD Press.

Herold, David M. and Donald B Fedor, *Change the Way You Lead Change: Leadership Strategies that Really Work,* 2008, Stanford Business Books.

Heskett, Jones, Loveman, Sasser, and Schlesinger, Putting the Service Profit Chain to Work, *Harvard Business Review,* 1994, Reprint Number 94204.

Kaufman, R. (2006). *Thirty Seconds That Can Change Your Life: A Decision-Making Guide for Those Who Refuse to Be Mediocre.* Amherst, MA: HRD Press, Inc.

Kaufman, R. (2006). Seven Stupid Things People Do When They Attempt Strategic Thinking and Planning, in Silberman, M., & Phillips, P. *The 2006 ASTD Organization Development & Leadership Sourcebook.* Alexandria, VA.

Kaufman, R. (2006, Aug.) Failure. What it is and how to invite it. *Performance Improvement. 45*(7), 9–12.

Kaufman, R. (2006). *Change, Choices, and Consequences: A Guide to Mega Thinking and Planning.* Amherst, MA: HRD Press, Inc.

Kaufman, R. (2000). *Mega Planning: Practical Tools for Organizational Success.* Thousand Oaks, CA. Sage Publications. Also *Planificación Mega: Herramientas practicas paral el exito organizacional.* (2004). Traducción de Sonia Agut. Universitat Jaume I, Castelló de la Plana, Espana.

Kaufman, R. (1998).*Strategic Thinking: A Guide to Identifying and Solving Problems. Revised.* Washington, DC & Arlington, VA: The International Society for Performance Improvement and the American Society for Training & Development. (Recipient of the 2001 International Society for Performance Improvement "Outstanding Instructional Communication Award.") Also, Spanish edition, *El Pensamiento Estrategico.* Centro De Estudios: Roman Areces, S.A., Madrid, Spain.

(http://www.elcorteingles.es/tiendas_e/cda/cera/producto/
0,5553,8480043660,FF.html).

Kaufman, R. (1992). *Strategic planning plus: An organizational
guide (Revised).* Newbury Park, CA: Sage Publishing.

Kaufman, R. & Bernardez, M. (2005) Eds. *Performance
Improvement_Quarterly,* Special invited issue on Mega
planning. Volume 18, Number 3. Pp. 3–5.
http://www.ispi.org/publications/ piqtocs/piq18_3.htm.

Krueger, Richard A., and Mary Anne Casey, *Focus Groups: A
Practical Guide for Applied Research,* 3rd Edition (2000),
Sage Publications Inc.

Patterson, Kerry, Joseph Grenny, David Maxfield, and Ron
McMillian, *Influencer: The Power to Change Anything,*
2007, McGraw-Hill

Waldrop, M. Mitchell, *Complexity: The Emerging Science at the
Edge of Order and Chaos,* 1992, Simon and Schuster.

Made in the USA
Coppell, TX
22 August 2024

36310582R00125